M000011987

GET REAL

GET
Real

THE POWER *of* GENUINE

LEADERSHIP, *a* TRANSPARENT

CULTURE, *and an* AUTHENTIC YOU

ANNA CROWE

LIONCREST
PUBLISHING

COPYRIGHT © 2019 ANNA CROWE

All rights reserved.

GET REAL

The Power of Genuine Leadership, a Transparent
Culture, and an Authentic You

ISBN   978-1-5445-0251-9 *Paperback*
            978-1-5445-0252-6 *Ebook*

To the younger version of me, who struggled so hard to be herself.

Also, to my husband and kids.

Contents

"Real isn't how you are made," said the Skin Horse. "It's a thing that happens to you. When a child loves you for a long, long time, not just to play with, but really loves you, then you become real."

"Does it hurt?" asked the Rabbit.

"Sometimes," said the Skin Horse, for he was always truthful. "When you are real you don't mind being hurt."

"Does it happen all at once, like being wound up," he asked, "or bit by bit?"

"It doesn't happen all at once," said the Skin Horse. "You become. It takes a long time. That's why it doesn't happen often to people who break easily, or have sharp edges, or who have to be carefully kept. Generally, by the time you are Real, most of your hair has been loved off, and your eyes drop out and you get loose in the joints and very shabby. But these things don't matter at all, because once you are Real you can't be ugly, except to people who don't understand."

—MARGERY WILLIAMS BIANCO,
THE VELVETEEN RABBIT

Introduction

The privilege of a lifetime is to become who you truly are.

—C. G. JUNG

It's no secret (or surprise) that professional environments look quite different today than they did two to three decades ago. Back then, people wanted—and needed—to be managed differently because they thought differently. Job satisfaction was nice to have, but it wasn't considered imperative. Work was a necessary part of life, and bringing home a steady paycheck was just as motivating for younger employees as it was for older ones. When people found a position that gave them a sense of security and satisfied their basic financial needs, they tended to stay put. Love it? No. But leave it? Never. Most employees' primary motivation in this antiquated working environment was the professional goals leadership set for them. The recognition of these goals through raises and promotions was viewed as the marker of success. Generations today (X, Y, Z, and everything in between) are motivated by so many other factors, including freedom, connections, the *why* behind their work, and the ability to fulfill their personal passions through work. *People are looking for authenticity in their lives and careers. They want to work for companies that value authenticity and allow them to flourish as individuals.*

This shift toward authenticity changes everything. When we were living in a goal-oriented business world, everything was done by the book, which meant every person in the company was managed in the same way. Little thought was given to who employees were as individuals, where they came from, how they might prefer to be managed, or what their unique gifts and aspirations were. For the younger generations in the workforce today, as well as those in older generations who have evolved with the times, this style is no longer effective. Companies who recognize this *and* do something about it are the ones that are flourishing.

For the often-cited Millennials (and now post-Millennials, known as Gen Z), a large part of job satisfaction hinges upon enjoying their day-to-day work life and engaging with their coworkers. These people want to feel like they can thrive in their work environment, not only materially, but also mentally and emotionally. Today's employees want to work in an atmosphere where they can create trust and build relationships. They want to show the world who they are and be accepted for their unique strengths, abilities, and even quirks. And those are just some of the reasons authenticity in the workplace is so important. There's no better way to facilitate trusting relationships than by breeding authenticity and transparency.

You've heard the old saying, "It's lonely at the top." In today's world, it can't be lonely at the top because we have to consider our entire team as cohorts in the trenches alongside us. Steve Jobs didn't create and grow Apple alone. As author Harvey McKay puts it, "Even the Lone Ranger didn't do it alone." To achieve meaningful and lasting success, organizations must focus on corporate culture, employee engagement, and employee happiness, in addition to the products or services they offer externally. Fostering authenticity among team members, within leadership, and as an integral part of your product or service is a big part of this.

Throughout my twenty-year career, I've worked for all sorts of different companies—big brands, startups, you name it. I've learned a ton of lessons and seen a variety of scenarios in the process. Recently, I decided to interview a handful of top-performing companies and business leaders, which you'll be hearing about in the pages to come. One thing I've noticed, both in my own experience and the experience of others, is that all successful businesses and leaders thrive by creating a culture of trust. In this sort of culture, employees of all levels are not afraid to speak the truth. They're not afraid to ask for help. Business leaders have begun to recognize a direct correlation between employee engagement and company success. Go figure.

Employees who work in authentic corporate environments feel freer to share their ideas, and tend to be more loyal and productive. There's little reason to look elsewhere for employment when they're happy, fulfilled, and see a clear growth path. Because employees understand where both their peers and management are coming from, and always know where they stand, conflict-ridden and superficial relationships fall by the wayside. This doesn't mean you have to be BFFs with your coworkers, but it does mean you should consider who they are as individuals. Everybody wins when each person can be him- or herself, and we can interact with one another as the unique people we are. This is how teams are created in the true sense of the word, not just corporate-speak.

AUTHENTIC TEAMS BUILD AUTHENTIC BRANDS

One thing I've noticed, both as an employee and as a

consultant, is that the same companies that breed transparency in their culture also tend to create the most authentic brands. Brand authenticity is becoming more important with each passing day, thanks to Instagram, Snapchat, and other social media outlets. We are more interconnected today than ever before. The more genuine a brand is, the better connection it can create with its customers.

Companies that haven't yet adapted to this new, genuine way of doing business present themselves as one thing, but are another in practice. Their mission isn't supported by their products, services, or culture. Today's customers are savvy enough to see through these discrepancies, and it's not a good look.

For a brand to be authentic, everything about it has to be real. This means *everything*—not just its core offering, but its mission, vision, and actions as well. If customers don't trust a brand, it doesn't matter what the product is, where it's sold, or how it's priced. A sustainable business cannot be built upon a foundation that isn't genuine.

Brand authenticity creates the building blocks of a trusting, long-term relationship with customers. It ensures that there will never be any confusion about "who" a company is and what it stands for. This doesn't mean that a business can't evolve and change, or do things differently over time. Every business should embrace innovation. However, what matters most is connecting with customers and creating trust. And the only way to do that is by—you guessed it—being authentic.

TYPES OF AUTHENTICITY IN BUSINESS

When we're talking about this concept in a corporate setting, we're looking at authenticity from several vantage points. We always begin with personal authenticity and extend outward from there. For the purposes of this book, we'll concentrate on four types of authenticity:

- Personal Authenticity
- Leadership Authenticity
- Corporate Culture Authenticity
- Brand Authenticity

PERSONAL AUTHENTICITY

Who are you? What matters most to you?

Personal authenticity is all about figuring out what makes you happy, what you want to do, and how to do it. To be clear, I'm not going to be talking about realizing your dream and living happily ever after. That's a topic worthy of another book. What I'm talking about is the opportunity for each one of us to better align our personal goals and our work with who we are at our core. It's how you can begin to approach work in a way that's more reflective of who you are, and in a way that makes you happier.

When you own who you are and feel more at ease and at home in your own skin, you have a far better chance of surrounding yourself with people who bring out the best in you. When you are more genuine in your personal life, it also extends to your professional life. You are better equipped to fulfill your potential, and more likely to be the person who lights up the room and inspires others.

LEADERSHIP AUTHENTICITY

How are you leading others to success?

Many business leaders are under the mistaken assumption that they have to put on a certain persona in order to command respect from their subordinates. Perhaps you think that to lead effectively you have to convey a certain presence or deliver your message in a way that intimidates.

Not only does this not work, but it's also not sustainable! And, I don't mean that in the environmentally unfriendly kind of way. It's not sustainable in the corporate environment. As a leader, you've got to build and nurture relationships and create trust. Meaningful relationships can only be developed when you lead as your true self, rather than presenting the "leadership version" of yourself.

CORPORATE CULTURE AUTHENTICITY

What type of culture and environment are you creating or contributing to?

When I see young leaders putting on a façade of leadership, it makes me question the corporate culture of their company. In a good, transparent culture, those at the highest level will embrace, develop, and create a safe space for those under them. They empower newcomers and young managers to be genuine. From this, we begin to see a trickle-down effect.

In a transparent, authentic company, a culture of sharing exists across the organization. The company understands that the more it shares its vision throughout all levels, the more engaged everyone is.

BRAND AUTHENTICITY

What does your brand truly stand for?

As important as it is for a company to be authentic in its culture, it's also important that it is authentic from an outward-facing perspective. Real companies create genuine brands. Customers engage in the most long-standing relationships with those brands because they're able to build a trusting connection with them.

You can have the most viral marketing campaign, garner millions of views for your product on social media, and earn yourself a ton of one-off sales. But if no one can remember the name of your product because your customers haven't formed a genuine connection with it, your success will be short-lived.

MY JOURNEY TO AUTHENTICITY

Like many people, I haven't always been able to show my true self to the world. Even now, there are days when I find it hard to be authentic 100 percent of the time. It can be really (*really*) tough. My deep interest in authenticity stems from my own personal and professional background. Born in Russia, I moved from Moscow to New York City with my family when I was eleven years old. I arrived knowing very little English aside from the basics. I had "Hello, my name is Anya," and "Happy birthday!" mastered. My tendency to sport hand-knit sweaters, acid-washed jeans, and Bart Simpson sneakers certainly did not help me blend in. From the moment I stepped into the sixth-grade classroom at PS 81 in the Bronx, it was clear that I did not fit in with my classmates. My time there was really, really, *really* awkward.

This was exacerbated by the fact that I was always the sort of student who really enjoyed school. I was that relentless (and, most likely, annoying) kid who sat in the front row and tried hard to resist the urge to answer every single question. The fact that I didn't know English didn't deter me. On that first day, I shot my hand up in the air to answer a question in—you guessed it—English class. When the teacher called on me, I scraped my chair back and proudly stood up. Laughter ensued. Not only did I look fresh off the boat and lack the correct vocabulary to answer the question, but I was shot down immediately for my etiquette as well. Until that moment, I had no idea that in America you continued lounging in your chair as you answered questions. Let's just say I didn't make that mistake again.

That first day at my new school was tough. In fact, that entire semester was tough. My ESL teacher told me she was concerned that I would never master the language. The problem wasn't that I couldn't learn, but that I was afraid to make a mistake. Rather than doing that, I acted as if I didn't understand. Needless to say, I felt culturally unfit and was afraid to speak up based on my first-day-of-school *faux pas*. Even worse than not fitting in, I didn't understand who I should be. I only understood that who I was wasn't right.

Over time, I learned to create a persona to get by. I laughed at jokes I didn't find funny and begged my mom to buy me the "right" clothes from the "right" places so that I looked like everyone else. It's no surprise that I didn't establish relationships that would stand the test of time at that school. How could I? I was putting on a performance of who I thought my classmates wanted me to be, rather than being who I was.

The only thing that kept me sane throughout my early years in America was the Russian school I attended at night. There, I got to hang out with people who were more like me and with whom I felt comfortable being myself. It was through this experience and the stark contrasts of my two worlds that I came to appreciate at a young age how incredibly important it is to find an environment where you can be yourself.

Despite these early lessons in personal authenticity, I still had a lot to learn when it came time to translate authenticity into my professional life. In college, I felt drawn toward fine arts and languages. But when my family asked what kind of job I could get in those fields, I didn't have a good answer. So, I followed a more pragmatic path and got into accounting. I was not a fan of most of my accounting classes, but I loved solving problems and being part of the business school, so I was happy enough. Also, the accounting degree at Rutgers Business School was considered one of the toughest at that time, so, being the studious person that I was, I took pleasure in being successful on a challenging path. That part was authentic to me.

After college, I immediately started working at a Fortune

100 accounting firm. It was a great opportunity and I loved the people around me, but it didn't feel quite like me. I spent most of my twenties trying out professional situations at a variety of companies and industries. After a few more years in Manhattan, I decided to get my MBA in international marketing and worked another three jobs, each of which moved me a little bit closer to work that felt "right." In those years, I moved from finance to marketing and sales and, finally, to where I am today, heading up a public relations company in Southern California. Go figure.

Where I ended up isn't where I saw myself heading twenty years ago. But by following those paths that seemed true to me, learning from them as I went, and using all the experiences along the way to propel me to the next step, I was able to find a corner of the business world that feels right and natural to me. It's like I was walking up a flight of stairs, but couldn't see the landing above me until I walked up the previous flight. It's all about moving up and looking ahead. It's a process of leveling up as your life and career evolve. I love my work now because it's true and it allows me to be authentic. I'm me when I'm at work.

From the outside looking in, my process of getting from there to here might look haphazard. Believe me, it wasn't easy. It was often equal parts tiring and thrilling to change direction. But for me, there was a method to the madness. I always chased things that made me excited to get out of bed in the morning. To me, happiness and success are getting to do what I love and surrounding myself with people who matter to me, whom I can work with to create change. I get bursts of energy when I have a new idea and experience great satisfaction when I get to put that idea into practice without boundaries. I try not to let failure distract me. Instead, I choose to see it as a growth opportunity and a way to eliminate one option. Most of my previous jobs didn't allow for the things that give those bursts of energy and excitement. I didn't want to live for the weekend. I wanted to live for every single day! *That's* my true self, and I wasn't going to feel fulfilled until I accomplished that.

A big reason I was able to make all of the leaps and transitions throughout the course of my career is because of the relationships I built. Every career opportunity came from genuine relationships I had created with people who happened to be influencers or decision-makers. The key to these relationships is that they developed from my genuine appreciation of these people, not because I was looking to network or make gains for myself. I invested in these people because I genuinely liked them and wanted to know and learn from them. They helped me along the way because, together, we had created a trusting relationship that allowed us to talk openly and honestly about what we really wanted out of our careers. In relationships like this, everyone wins. When we connect on a genuine level, we can problem-solve together, and each party can take away some value.

What I've also learned throughout the years is that these relationships aren't limited to coworkers and colleagues. We can also build strong relationships with our clients and others who come into our lives. We can establish symbiotic, trusting relationships wherein our clients realize that we're *humans* doing business together. Part of building these client relationships is the willingness to own up to things that aren't working. Through honesty, trust is established, communication is enhanced, and a true connection is cultivated.

BUILDING AUTHENTICITY

In the pages that follow, we'll examine the four types of authenticity in the workplace. We'll discover how they build upon one another, beginning with personal authenticity and extending all the way to brand authenticity.

We'll see how everything in our professional life is improved when we cultivate authenticity. Our levels of personal satisfaction increase; we build better relationships with coworkers and clients; we're better leaders; productivity and sustainability skyrocket; and we gain the loyalty of customers and clients alike.

What you'll read in this book isn't rocket science. I didn't invent this concept, nor am I solving the world's biggest issues. In fact, there's a good chance you already know why authenticity matters, and you're here looking for a few tools that will enable you to be your best self and to inspire others around you. You've come to the right place.

Being yourself can be scary sometimes—especially in those moments when being yourself requires you to be vulnerable. But as you'll see, it's so worth it.

CHAPTER ONE

Authenticity Comes of Age

You attract the right things when you have a sense of who you are.

—AMY POEHLER

Authenticity is a #trending buzzword these days. In the time it's taken me to write this book, it seems as if people are talking about authenticity more and more. Or perhaps I'm more sensitive to it now. Despite all of these conversations, many people still aren't exactly sure what authenticity means. Probably because it tends to mean different things to different people.

For the purposes of this book, think of authenticity as staying true to your values and yourself. Authenticity allows you to communicate your thoughts and ideas without filtering them based on concern about what others might think. Most of all, authenticity means not being someone or something you're not. In this book, we'll focus on what this looks like in business and organizational environments. When you act from a place of authenticity, you are able to find more fulfillment and success in your career and in your business.

Despite the sometimes nebulous nature of the word "authenticity," I think most of us understand what it means to be ourselves. The problem comes with this quirk of human nature that makes us fearful of acting on who we genuinely are. This fear can arise for a number of reasons, such as the fear of being judged, or the notion that you have to put up a front for your peers, managers, or subordinates. Since most of us have an innate understanding of what it would look like to be ourselves, but many of us still aren't actually doing so, we're making a *choice* not to be authentic. Why is this?

THE VULNERABILITY OF AUTHENTICITY

When we are being true to ourselves, we are also being vulnerable. Authenticity has elements of both courage and emotion. Often, it's much easier to give people the answers they want than it is to be direct and say what you are really thinking, feeling, or wanting. If someone disagrees with or laughs at you, what does that say about you? To be authentic, you have to cast aside your fears of all this. As *The Magic of Thinking Big* author, David Schwartz, puts it, "Action cures fear, inaction creates terror."

Being authentic might require more courage and vulnerability in some cases than others. It certainly does in those moments when you're called upon to show your true colors and those colors aren't so pretty. Or when authenticity requires you to wear your heart on your sleeve. Authenticity may not always be the easy choice; however, it's usually the *best* choice.

I recently got into a great discussion about the relationship between authenticity and vulnerability with a good friend of mine, CBS reporter Ashley Jacobs. As we dug into our charcuterie board over lunch, Ashley addressed the importance of vulnerability in a way that I think most of us can relate to:

> I think people are so fearful of rejection that they'd rather live a lie than be accepted for being less than perfect. It's not always easy to admit shortcomings (nor is it always necessary), but learning to know when to admit you're wrong, when to fight for something you believe in, and when to show your true self, is an art we can all work on. Authenticity is crucial for gaining trust. When others can trust in you, they believe in you, and you will succeed.

Ashley brings up another important point about authenticity, which is that it leads you along the life path that is most true to you. It asks you to understand who you are, and to act from that place. This is a process that can take years. However, there are few other things in life that are as worthy of this effort. You may find these answers in your relationships, your career, your hobbies, or any other number of arenas. It doesn't matter where or what it is. The important thing is that you figure it out.

PEOPLE VS. PERSONAS

Once you've chiseled down to the heart of who you are, the next step is allowing the world to see and interact with that true version of you. Particularly in this age of social media, we have become accustomed to putting a persona of ourselves out into the world as opposed to our true selves.

This isn't to say that it's not okay to be aspirational, because it is. But don't be afraid to present the other facets of yourself to the world as well—good, bad, and ugly. It's human nature to believe that others won't like or respect you as much if they can see the parts of you that are less than ideal, but the opposite is often true.

Take Virgin Group founder Richard Branson, for example. As many others around the globe also do, I've admired him from afar for years for a slew of reasons. Branson is the only person in the world to have built eight separate billion-dollar companies from scratch in eight different countries. And do you know what Branson cites as one of his secrets to success? Dyslexia. Yes, a learning disorder is his greatest strength, and he's not shy about telling people. In fact, if you follow him on social media, you'll know that, in addition to discussing his companies' successes, innovation, and inspirational messages, Branson also shares very real and personal issues, including his failures and major life moments. Because of this, we can relate to him as a person, which makes us feel as if we can relate to and trust what his company does as well.

The ability to be forthcoming is admirable. We all have unique skills, and we also have flaws. Without the vulnerability he brings to the table, a billionaire like Branson would be almost impossible to connect with because it would feel like he was some sort of superhuman, as if he had his own playing field, completely separate from ours. It's no accident that many of the most influential people in the world share this same quality of owning their whole self—people such as Oprah Winfrey and Barack Obama. Speaking about her own learning curve with authenticity, Oprah says, "I had no idea that being your authentic self could make me as rich as I've become. If I had, I'd have done it a lot earlier."

Without this ownership of your entire self, changing and

evolving becomes much more difficult. If people don't know what your weaknesses are, how can they contribute to your growth? This is particularly relevant in the workplace. When you are brave and vulnerable enough to be straightforward with your boss about where you want to grow, they can help facilitate this. They will also be in a better position to recognize your growth and the effort you're putting forth when you start from an honest place.

To embrace authenticity in all aspects of your life, you need to drop the persona. Knowing who you are is not enough. You also have to bring that person into the world. Let the world see who you are, what you want to do, and how you want to do it.

PERSONAS IN TODAY'S BUSINESS WORLD

Thanks to social media and generational mindset shifts, your bosses and coworkers have an unprecedented glimpse into who you are outside of working hours. Even a decade ago, it was much easier to separate into two distinct selves: your professional self and your personal self. This is increasingly less true. It is also more obvious than ever before when you are presenting a persona at work. When you're making a practice of this, that pending friend or follow request can put you in a tough spot.

However, no matter how pervasive social media is or how

transparent Millennials and Gen Zers tend to be, work is still work. You want to be your true self at work, but with the understanding that work will always require a level of professionalism. You want to strike that balance between being appropriately professional and still remaining yourself and playing up your strengths.

GENERATIONAL SHIFTS

Today's workforce meshes together Boomers, Gen Xers, Millennials, and Gen Zers. Although Millennials are increasingly entering the ranks of upper management, those higher-echelon positions still tend to consist mainly of Gen Xers and Boomers. Because of this, the dynamics of business leaders are sometimes quite different than those of the younger employees they're managing.

Today, much of life is broadcast on social media. If it didn't make it to social, did it really happen? Regardless of what generation you belong to, you are probably connected to some of your coworkers on social media. Even if you're not, you're still searchable enough that your coworkers are able to easily get a glimpse into your personal life if they want to. Because of this, it is increasingly difficult to be one person at work and another outside of work without appearing fake or inauthentic. If your coworkers sense this, developing true and trusting relationships becomes more of an uphill battle.

The transparency of our lives in the digital world has had a trickle-down effect on how we interact in real life. Particularly in the case of startups and small businesses, hierarchy looks much different than it used to. The division between ranks isn't as strict as it once was, which is largely a good thing. I see this breakdown of "old" norms and boundaries in my own office, where interns feel free to come into my office and ask me questions directly. When I was an intern twenty years ago, I never could have walked into my boss's office unannounced.

This breakdown of hierarchy is indicative of the fact that young people demand more than a superficial connection with managers and coworkers. This personal connection is an integral piece of job satisfaction, and it entails more than just respecting and being respected by coworkers. It involves cultivating actual relationships. When individuals are unwilling to engage in anything beyond professional discourse, Millennials and Gen Zers begin to feel as if something is being hidden from them. They suspect a lack of transparency, which results in a breakdown of trust.

What if you are a reserved person who doesn't feel comfortable sharing the more personal details of your life with coworkers? What if that kind of sharing isn't authentic to who you are? Of course, no one should ever feel forced to disclose more than they want to or more than they feel is appropriate in a professional work setting. Doing something that doesn't come naturally to you can easily cross over into inauthenticity, so I don't recommend pushing yourself to share everything.

Luckily, there are other ways to build trust and connection beyond sharing the intimate personal details of your life in a way that might not feel comfortable for you. Often, you can accomplish the same results by showing vulnerability. This signifies to others that you are comfortable with and trust them. Vulnerability doesn't mean you have to cry at the office. You can be vulnerable by doing something as simple as telling someone that you admire a certain quality of theirs or sharing a situation in which you've failed.

For leaders, giving honest, direct feedback is also vulnerable and can help strengthen connections, even though that might seem counterintuitive. Strong leaders are willing to have tough conversations even when it feels uncomfortable to address the issue. It's often easier to brush off an issue in the moment. The problem is that these smaller issues and incidents continue to stack up until they compound into something much bigger that has to be addressed. When it finally is, the employee is caught off guard. They didn't even know anything was wrong! We'll look at some strategies for making these conversations as effective as possible in chapter 4.

By showing those who report to you that you will always give authentic, in-the-moment feedback—both good and bad—you are building their trust in you. You are showing them where they stand. I've learned this same lesson many times over years of working with Millennials—they want real-time feedback. If they have faith in you and trust that you're being genuine in your analysis, that's plenty. They know they can come to you when they need to. They will respect you, which will motivate them to get the job done. You are now a real person rather than an inaccessible persona of "boss" or "manager."

A CULTURE OF TRANSPARENCY

When we cultivate authentic interactions among coworkers, we create the building blocks for a positive, productive, transparent corporate culture. Transparency doesn't just make us feel good about our connection with coworkers; it also plays a pragmatic role in good business. It can create a strong corporate culture, and increase employee engagement, customer loyalty, and productivity.

Businesses have a huge competitive advantage when their employees are adaptable and growth-oriented. When you are transparent with feedback, you allow for growth. This serves the employee, but it also serves the greater purpose of creating a healthy company.

When you provide feedback within a transparent, safe culture, you help employees grow and evolve without alienating them in the process. With transparency, employees understand that leadership is on their side, even when managers are providing constructive criticism.

I was recently on a conference call with a client, one of my managers, and a star junior staff member. This junior staff member—who shall remain nameless—is engaged, passionate, and aligned with our company's mission and vision. She's awesome. But on this particular call, I couldn't help but notice that she wasn't at her best. In fact, she sounded like her car had just been rear-ended right before she hopped on the phone. Even though the call went fine overall, I couldn't help but think this interaction probably didn't give our client the best impression of our company—or of this woman. She just wasn't presenting herself as the rock star she is.

I had plenty to do after the call, so I could have easily brushed this aside and ignored the meeting as a one-off. Or I could have set our conversation aside for days or weeks later, and then told her the performance was unacceptable. Instead, when the call ended, I pulled the woman's manager aside and asked if she had noticed the same thing. Perhaps my perception was somehow clouded. We agreed that she was capable of much more. Her genuine energy and enthusiasm didn't shine through.

Perhaps there was something happening in her life that we needed to be aware of. Or perhaps she just didn't notice how she was presenting herself in this situation.

We agreed that the manager would have an open conversation with her, with the goal of creating a safe space to communicate and find a solution. If there was something serious happening in her life, it would continue to impact her professional performance, so we needed to get to the *why*.

It turned out that, in this particular case, the employee was simply unaware of the fact that she was coming across as disengaged, and she was appreciative of the conversation and the feedback. It allowed her to be more aware of how she was presenting herself. Because we had cultivated a safe, transparent environment and approached the discussion with her as a way of helping rather than reprimanding, she was able to view the feedback in a positive light. This allows us to improve as a company and grow as individuals. We walk away stronger because we're able to support and help one another grow into our full potential.

ROOM FOR DIFFERENCES

When a corporate culture is built around transparency and authenticity, it takes into account the fact that everyone works differently, has different strengths, and offers a unique perspective. How you work best with one person may not be how you work best with someone else. Employees are allowed and encouraged to understand one another on a deeper level, and to connect within specific, unique parameters that actually work.

For example, one of my former managers was known for her BGG policy—be brief, be good, be gone. We all knew that when we had an issue to discuss with her, we needed to be eloquent and quick. There was never any confusion about how to most effectively interact with her, because the culture was transparent and honesty was encouraged. Our feelings weren't hurt because of the fact that conversations weren't drawn out.

We also understood that other people in the office didn't enjoy working in such an abrupt manner. Some people required a more personal connection and wanted to spend more time lingering over discussions and making small talk. For them, more interaction ultimately created a better outcome than a brief, to-the-point encounter.

By encouraging a culture in which everyone is allowed to connect and let their personalities and preferences be known, the company becomes more effective and successful. It allows everyone to work in the way that suits them best, rather than forcing everyone into a single, uniform mold.

UNITED IN VISION AND MESSAGE

Allowing everyone's unique personalities to shine through results in a stronger company. However, the one element that everyone should be single-minded about is the company's vision. The vision has to feel authentically meaningful to each employee, because it is their collective belief and genuine buy-in that will result in an authentic business.

If you are an environmentalist working for a company that's innovating sustainable technology, chances are you are going to be invested in that company in a very organic way. Multiply this enthusiasm by all of the employees, and you've got one killer company on your hands. However, if you have a bunch of vegans working for a meat-processing plant, clearly, they're not buying into the company's vision, and that inauthenticity will be clear. Can they still do a great job? Definitely. But will they be invested in the company's growth and fully embrace their day-to-day duties and the people around them? Not likely. Consumers are far savvier than we give them credit for, and they have an innate sense of what is real.

It's also important that companies and brands support

any claims they're making through their actions. They need to deliver on the messaging they're putting out into the world. This is how the public will gauge transparency and authenticity, and build trust. For example, if my company talks about supporting charitable endeavors, but takes no action, consumers are going to recognize that and call all of my company's claims into question.

To connect with the outside world, it's important for companies to stay true to their vision. Many companies have to pivot as the world and the global marketplace evolve and change. That's good business—as long as the company is pivoting with its vision in mind.

What companies should *never* do is try to be something they're not. Personas are no more sustainable for companies than they are for human beings. Every consumer-facing component of business, from its products and services to how it interacts within the community, must come from a place that reflects what the company stands for.

A vision is just words on a piece of paper. What brings it to life are actions. Over time, a series of actions that bolster this vision add up to a reputation for authenticity. Consumers will see through everything else, and customers do not want to support companies they don't trust. What's more, they don't have to when so many different options are just a few keystrokes away.

As recently as a decade ago, it was possible for business-people to separate life and work, and for companies to hide behind slogans. Today, generational shifts and technology have blurred the lines and lifted the veil like never before.

It seems counterintuitive at first, but the technology that is now integral to both our personal and professional lives *also* requires that we bring more humanity to the table.

Vulnerability, transparency, and authenticity are even more critical today than they've ever been before.

CHAPTER TWO

Cultivating Genuine Habits

Authenticity is a collection of choices that we have to make every day. It's about the choice to show up and be real. The choice to be honest. The choice to let our true selves be seen.

—BRENÉ BROWN

Even if you understand what authenticity is, that still doesn't necessarily make it comfortable to be authentic 100 percent of the time. Some of us are lucky if we can achieve a 50 percent success rate. This is nothing more than being human. The good news is that there are some simple steps we can take to incorporate more authenticity into our lives.

THE FIVE CORE HABITS OF AUTHENTICITY

You already know what it means to be genuine. Now it's

time to put that skill into practice. It might be uncomfortable at first but, over time, it will get easier. With enough practice, it will become instinctive.

Being more genuine is a habit we can practice, just like anything else. I've identified five core habits that lead to a more authentic lifestyle. As is always the case with building habits, small steps and consistent behavior result in change over the long term.

The habits I've identified can help you become more comfortable sharing and communicating what's natural and real to you. Most importantly, they'll help you bring into the world something that no one else has to offer—you!

HABIT 1: BE HUMAN

Artificial intelligence may be all the rage these days, but there's no substitute for humanity and emotion. Although it might sound counterintuitive, it is our vulnerability that is our greatest superpower as human beings.

Vulnerability allows us to showcase both our strengths and our weaknesses. In fact, researcher Brené Brown views vulnerability and authenticity as inextricably intertwined. When we are vulnerable, we can become comfortable with *all* aspects of ourselves. This also allows us to be more compassionate to the world around us.

When we recognize that we have our differences from everyone around us—and, moreover, when we embrace these unique traits—we begin to realize that the same is equally true for others. There is no one-size-fits-all model.

Particularly in the business world, it's easy to worry that others will view our humanity and vulnerability as weakness. I believe the opposite is true. Whether you're the CEO of a major corporation, an investor, an intern, a celebrity, or a Nobel Peace Prize winner, we all connect with one another as human beings. This connection becomes easier when we show our vulnerability. Vulnerability reminds others that you are human, just like them. You, too, have insecurities, passions, desires, and goals.

We seem to have made a silent collective agreement to "fake it till we make it." Many people hide behind this veneer, afraid to speak up about those skills they have not yet mastered and the information they don't yet have. We're all afraid that we're going to disappoint someone. Maybe you're scared that if you let others realize what you don't yet know, you'll lose your job. Or perhaps you have a more general fear that others will have a negative impression of you if you don't know the answer to something. No matter how much we might claim otherwise, most of us care what others think about us.

The irony of all of this is that we are *all* human. Showing this humanity shouldn't be as difficult as it often seems. Somehow we've all bought into the myth that we are expected to be superhuman and appear invincible. In an effort to do this, we create masks and layers to cover up that very thing that connects us to one another.

This is why you have to show your humanity, even if you feel like no one around you is doing the same. I bet you'll find that the more human and more vulnerable you are, the more human and vulnerable those around you will also be. No one wants to work for or with robots. Maybe that won't be the case twenty years from now when AI takes over, but for now, the people around you crave human connection just as much as you do. They just might not know how to come out and say it. You can pave the path for them.

Both inside and outside of work, connecting with others on a personal level can be scary. It's like we create these imaginary hierarchical boundaries to create a safe space where there are fewer threats of the unknown. We worry that if these boundaries are eroded, our true self will be revealed. We fear that, with this, we will lose whatever sense of power and control we might have. Every time you feel these fears creep up, try to remember that everyone else has all of these same anxieties.

If you're a parent, you're probably all too well aware of the fact that consistency is key. When you make a decision or set a rule, you have to stick with it. Otherwise, chaos ensues. This is just as true in the rest of life as it is with parenting.

For instance, one of the key rules in branding, marketing, and PR is that you must maintain a consistent message so that people know what—and who—to expect. There's so much noise out there in this digital world of ours that if you are constantly changing your message, people won't know who you are or what you stand for. Their trust will erode and so will their likes, follows, and purchases. You can either be Dr. Jekyll or Mr. Hyde—but you have to choose one.

Consistency is your primary way of allowing others to understand where they stand with you. If you're tough, great! Be consistently tough. But if you're not, don't pretend to be because you think that will get the necessary response. Use your strengths and genuine actions to get what you need. The truth is that pretense is way more transparent and less effective than you believe it to be. When people sniff out subterfuge, they won't believe what you're saying and you'll lose their respect.

I once worked for someone who was quite abrasive in

her delivery. Whenever I submitted work for review, she would unfailingly provide honest, candid feedback. And it wasn't pretty. At first, it felt excessive. Sometimes, it felt downright mean. But at the end of the day, I knew what to expect from her, and I knew that whatever she said was legit. If she was hard on me, I knew it was because she knew I could do better. She knew I had to improve. In the end, I appreciated her consistency and authenticity, because I always knew where I stood and what to expect from her. Her honesty and approach taught me how to deal with feedback better, and enabled me to learn faster and grow personally and professionally.

Once you crack through the fear, it's always easiest to just be yourself. It requires so much less effort because, by definition, being yourself comes naturally. When you are yourself, you are guaranteed to achieve the ultimate consistency. Personas are never consistent.

I've noticed that one of the key symptoms of putting on a façade is an inability to communicate effectively. I used to work with someone who was very pleasant and warm when she walked through the office and interacted with employees one-on-one. Her emails, on the other hand, were passive-aggressive missiles. It was jarring to have a pleasant "good morning" chat, followed up by a passive-aggressive email three minutes later. This inconsistent communication style was confusing and created an uncomfortable working environment. Inconsistency negatively impacts everyone's performance, the level of respect among coworkers, and business as a whole.

Consistency in the workplace is achieved in two ways: first, by understanding who you are, and second, by *being* who you are. New young managers often feel they have to demonstrate authority in any way possible. For some, that means being tough or even brutal; for others, it means emulating their own boss's style, whether it also works for them or not. Copying behavior may be the highest form of flattery, but it's not sustainable and only creates confusion.

Any new manager's first step should be self-examination. How do I want to lead? What kind of leader do I want to be? Self-examination leads to self-awareness, and to an understanding of what works for you.

The clearer you are about who you are—both with yourself and with others—the more compelling and effective you will be as a leader. Also, clarity leads to a direct approach, which everyone can embrace.

HABIT 3: STAND BEHIND YOUR WORD

It's this simple: if you say something, stand behind it. How many times has an acquaintance talked about getting together, and even as you nod and smile in response, you know that person has no intention of following through? There are a lot of words floating around out there in the world as it is. You don't need to add to them with more words that can't be substantiated by action. If you're going to say it, mean it. Then do it.

Like all of us, I'm sure that you often have the best intentions, even when you don't follow through. We all sometimes make claims that we don't have the ability to substantiate or support. The best way to break this habit is by taking small steps.

Be realistic about your capabilities so that you can set the correct expectations. This is especially important in the corporate environment. If you tell an employee that they will be promoted if they deliver on a particular project, and then change the criteria once that assignment is finished, everyone will lose faith in your word. When you say you'll have a project delivered by a certain date, deliver it by that date. It's okay to say, "I can't do that," when it's the truth. It's way better to be honest about what you are incapable of than to say you can do something you can't. When you ask something of others or tell them you are going to do something, they will believe you—until they have a reason not to. If you continuously disappoint, you will lose the trust of others.

This doesn't mean that you have to write all of your intentions down in permanent marker. Let's be real: if everyone did that, we would all fail miserably on a daily basis. However, when you're communicating with people about things that really matter to them, such as a promotion or deadline, you have to follow through to the greatest extent and as often as possible. There are few things more difficult than earning back someone's trust once you've lost it.

HABIT 4: REMEMBER IT'S OKAY NOT TO KNOW

It's okay that you don't have all of the answers—in fact, it's a sign of strength. There seems to be a rampant misconception that if we don't have an immediate answer or solution for every question we're asked and issue we're faced with, we're somehow flawed. Of course, this isn't true. We're human, and not a single person among us knows everything. Strong leaders don't waste their time and energy hiding weaknesses; instead, they focus on getting better and stronger. Even people who appear superhuman, like Elon Musk and Jeff Bezos, don't have all the answers.

It's okay to show others that you're in the same position as they are, and to demonstrate through example that it's okay to search for answers and to strive for improvement in the process. The ability to ask for help is a big key to emotional intelligence. One of the best things you can do as a leader (or an up-and-coming leader) is to demonstrate to employees that it's okay to ask questions.

When one of my employees asks me how to solve a problem I haven't faced before, and I don't have an immediate solution, I freely admit it. But I let them know that we will figure it out and create a game plan for getting that answer. This conveys the message that it's okay to not know everything, and that we still have the ability to find a solution. This sort of answer also empowers others to solve problems and fosters a collaborative spirit. Talk about a great way to build confidence and team power! Everyone wins.

Don't get me wrong. This doesn't mean that it's okay to be unqualified or dishonest about your abilities because you figure you can learn information that's critical to your job at some point down the line. Honesty and vulnerability should simply be part of your character, so that when you interview for a position, you can be upfront and confident in your responses. I once hired an intern who professed to be masterful at working with social influencers in her interview. We were in a rush to hire at that time, and didn't do all of the necessary due diligence on our end to verify this fact. Once she was hired and asked to source three social influencers, she couldn't think of one.

On the other hand, when I asked another candidate about her experience with social influencers, she responded, "You know, I haven't worked with them, but I've done similar work, and I'm confident that I can figure it out, based on my past experience." She proceeded to explain her strategy for learning about and connecting with influencers. We hired her, with a clear and realistic understanding about her baseline. Rather than being disappointed in the long run, the team was pleasantly surprised when she followed her strategy and picked up the information she needed to do her job well.

Knowing it all is not important, but transparency is.

HABIT 5: OWN YOUR MISTAKES

Mistakes are going to happen. They're a fact of life. Most of the time, we don't even see our mistakes until they've been made. Most of the time, they can be remedied.

When you make a mistake, the first step is to own it. Then, devise a strategy for fixing it. Finally, ask yourself what you can take away from the experience. Believe it or not, leaders make mistakes constantly. Every day. It's an integral part of growing and building knowledge. Sometimes they're big mistakes, and sometimes they're small, inconsequential ones. The best part of mistakes is that we can learn from them and avoid the same pitfalls in the future.

As Winston Churchill put it, "Success is stumbling from failure to failure with no loss of enthusiasm."

If you never admit to being wrong at work and are always coming up with excuses or blaming someone else, you risk creating division. Coworkers will begin to wonder why you never make mistakes when they make them all the time. On the other hand, when you own your mistakes and use them as a learning opportunity, you can easily transform negatives into positives. Others will learn from you, and they won't be afraid to own their errors. When everyone is honest and accountable, situations can be remedied more quickly, and they won't escalate into much larger mistakes.

For instance, in a crisis situation, a forthright executive who owns their mistake, addresses it, and makes an immediate plan to fix it regains trust faster than one who hides behind blanket statements. It's not just companies, public figures, and corporate executives who benefit from this strategy. Yes, time is of the essence when you make a mistake, but being forthright about it is half the battle.

It's helpful to be in an environment that enables you to remedy the situation, and to work with team members who will support you in the process. This is why working in a corporate culture that promotes transparency is so important. If you're not in this sort of environment, you should still be as forthright as possible. Perhaps you can even lead the way toward changing the culture for the better.

Attempting to cover up mistakes rarely works. Once you're found out, the risk of losing respect of others is great. This includes not making excuses. Good excuses are just lies wrapped up in reason.

Finally, remember that, just as you should own your mistakes, you should also own your accomplishments. It's the same process—be direct about it in order to save your time and energy, as well as the time and energy of those around you.

Efficiency with these matters puts both you and those you work with on a forward path. We live in a fast-paced society, and we're expected to accomplish more in less time. Why waste valuable time with excuses when you can simply move on and fix the situation?

NETFLIX: A MASTER COURSE IN NAVIGATING MISTAKES

Netflix offers a prime example in mistake ownership. Over a series of years, Netflix went from being a DVD mailing service to a streaming service as well. One day in 2011, seemingly out of the blue, Netflix announced they were doing away with their $10 combined DVD and streaming membership and raising their rates by nearly 60 percent, to $15.98 for two separate services. The public freaked out. The company lost more than 1 million customers, and their stock plummeted by 77 percent in just four months. A lot of people—myself included—figured that was the end of Netflix. Some referred to this corporate disaster as Netflixodus.

The company had to course-correct and alleviate the anger of customers. Netflix CEO Reed Hastings posted a blog overturning the decision to split the business and openly offered a mea culpa about the company's pricing decisions. "I messed up," he stated plainly. "In hindsight, I slid into arrogance based upon past success."

Of course, Netflix is still around and stronger than ever despite their snafu. Granted, they didn't turn things around based solely on this statement, but I strongly believe that the reason they made it through the backlash is because their apology was so honest and transparent. Who among us doesn't relate to or connect with overstepping?

Yes, Netflix is a company and a brand, but it humanized itself—and, arguably, ultimately deepened its connection with customers—by admitting its error in straightforward and relatable language. Because of this, customers are more loyal than ever, and Netflix is more profitable than ever. Netflix embodies the idea that authenticity is a competitive advantage.

THE PAYOFF

None of these habits are rocket science, but putting them into practice can be easier said than done in the moment. It's tough to grow as a person, and it's also tough to climb the corporate ladder. Sometimes putting your best foot forward means trying to substantiate your claims any way you know how. Just remember that there's a huge difference between *appearing* better than you are and *working toward* being better than you are.

We often turn to inauthenticity when things become stressful, whether emotionally or logistically. However, the truth is, putting on a façade is incredibly stressful, too. Not to mention the fact that it almost always backfires. There's no shortcut to hard work, so spare yourself unnecessary time, energy, and stress, and concentrate on being more genuine. Put your effort toward being a better, truer version of yourself, rather than a different version of yourself.

CHAPTER THREE

Personal Authenticity

Authenticity is more than speaking; authenticity is also about doing. Every decision we make says something about who we are.

—SIMON SINEK

Perhaps authenticity doesn't rank as one of the top priorities on your never-ending list of to-dos or things to achieve. But I'm willing to bet happiness is somewhere up there.

I can't tell you that I have discovered the magical key to happiness. But I do know that I have found certain situations that, without fail, result in a more positive, fulfilling experience. There is a direct correlation between happiness and these certain situations.

Happiness is cultivated through the way you live your life every single day. To be sustainable, happiness must be rooted in simplicity—and I'm not talking about tiny houses or a disconnected life (although that is happiness for many). When you live life in a way that's in line with your beliefs—in other words, authentically—everything is so much simpler.

Being yourself means that your energy and attention are focused on what really matters, rather than being wasted on creating superficial layers. It means taking action in ways that fulfill and resonate with you. It means putting your attention toward those endeavors that motivate you and keep your interest. Or it means that, at least, you are on the way to doing these things.

Surrounding yourself with people who like you for *you* also breeds happiness. The best relationships require the least amount of effort. Constantly putting on a front or trying to impress others is exhausting. Relationships thrive when you are able to let your guard down. As we've already discussed, relationships are critical to our success and happiness because human beings naturally seek connection.

DESTINATION: SELF-AWARENESS

The one common denominator necessary to cultivate all

of the scenarios linked with happiness is self-awareness. Self-awareness allows you to understand with great clarity the values you hold dear. A self-aware person understands how they communicate best, the type of environment they thrive in, how they come across to others, and their baseline for emotional fulfillment.

If you've ever done any work to improve a past or current relationship (and who hasn't?), you may have heard about the concept of love languages. This theory, written about by author Gary Chapman in *The Five Love Languages*, argues that there are five primary modes of giving and receiving love. Each of us tends to gravitate toward one or two of those languages. Once we understand which language we speak, we have a greater understanding of what we need to feel loved. Sounds easy enough.

Self-awareness is similar. Once we recognize our own language of self-awareness and understand what makes us tick, we can be more genuine.

Still, it's a process. Self-awareness won't necessarily come in the form of huge lightning-bolt epiphanies about yourself. It can just as easily be the result of an accumulation of small tidbits of information you realize about yourself along the way. The trick is to learn how to collect these discoveries, and then put them to use to live a happier life.

For example, many people dream of someday moving to a big city like New York. They are drawn to it for the career opportunities, excitement, cool factor, or any number of other reasons. Once they actually arrive in New York, many of these people find that the city isn't the right fit for them. Everyone has a different journey. Just because you see something work for others, doesn't mean it will work for you. You can spend hours, days, or even years pondering a decision or building something up in your mind. But more often than not, you don't know what will or won't work for you until you actually do it.

We're humans, and none of us is perfect. But it's perfectly okay to make a wrong call in life. In fact, making mistakes or decisions that don't work out can even be a good thing. The key is to use these experiences to put together the puzzle that is you. Not all of the pieces you pick up will fit. That's fine, because now you can cast that piece aside and concentrate on finding the piece that *does* fit. I've cast aside hundreds of "wrong" pieces in my own life, all of which have helped me find the right ones. I don't have to worry about the ones I set aside, because I've tried them and they just don't fit.

Trial and error is an extremely helpful and even necessary part of the journey toward self-awareness. How can you know what you like or dislike until you try it out? You can make an educated guess, but nothing is guaranteed. Also, not trying something out often only leaves you with more uncertainty and questions. You can't know that you will like a career or location until you give it a shot. Even if it turns out not to be the right fit for you, at least now you know what you don't like about it. This will lead you one step closer to figuring out what you do like.

CREATE YOUR ROADMAP

Most people don't sit down and think about where they want to be in the next year, five years, or decade. That's okay—life gets busy, and there's a lot of beauty in living in the moment. But there's also great value in taking a step back to get an overview of your life. As Arnold Schwarzenegger once said in an interview, "If you have a very clear vision of where you want to go, then the rest of it is much easier." Coming from a former leading competitive bodybuilder turned real estate mogul turned movie star turned governor, I would say there's a lot of value in his outlook.

Take a few minutes right now and visualize the roadmap toward your ideal future. Where are you right now? Where do you want to go? What steps can you take to bring more happiness and satisfaction into your life on a daily basis? What might you do to cultivate more long-term happiness? The size of the steps does not matter in the grand scheme of life. What matters is that you're continuously moving, improving, and shifting toward those goals.

The potential answers and possibilities are endless. For you, happiness might involve a new car or a beautiful house. It might involve a new relationship or a promotion. Perhaps, for you, happiness lies in making more time for hobbies or saving up to travel a few years from now. It doesn't matter what your answers are. Don't judge whether they seem superficial or selfish. The only important thing is that they resonate with and are true to you. Your map should be a reflection of you, your dreams, and your desires. The "locations" on that map should evoke happiness.

One of the most important elements of this roadmap of yours is the things that will bring you daily happiness. It's these little moments of pleasure in day-to-day life that will keep you excited about what you're doing and create the momentum to drive you toward your long-term vision. For most people, that happy-inducing element will align with their values, interests, and skillset.

Following this roadmap doesn't mean that every day will be filled with butterflies and rainbows. It *does* mean that you shouldn't start counting down to Friday evening as soon as your alarm goes off on Monday morning.

Wasting even a day of your life is no small matter. Those

days are limited in number, and every single day offers us a new opportunity to make changes for the better. If you are unhappy with some element of your life, find the avenues and outlets that will lead you closer to more enjoyment. Use those outlets as little pathways that will ultimately lead to the destination of your vision of happiness.

Finally, always remember that choosing not to do anything at all to change a situation that is unfulfilling or doesn't make you happy is just that—a *choice*. Ultimately, it is a choice that will keep you stuck right where you are.

TAKE ACTION

Coming to new understandings about yourself and creating a plan isn't enough. You also have to put that information into action.

I started my career in public accounting at Deloitte, a Big 4 (then Big 5) accounting firm. It didn't take very long for me to realize that I loved a challenge, client relations, and working on teams. I also realized that I needed to work for a company I believed in. While I enjoyed the people I worked with, I wasn't passionate about my day-to-day tasks, such as auditing financial statements, reconciling accounts, and spending months on end traveling. I enjoyed learning new things, but didn't feel like I was maximizing my potential. So, I stayed for two years, then took the opportunity to use these new pieces of information I'd discovered about myself as a chance to learn even more. I was now armed with the information I needed to find a job that allowed me to do more of what I loved and less of what I didn't.

My next job also involved financial analysis, but this time I worked in-house for a major cosmetics and fragrance company in New York City. I discovered that I loved working with and on brands. I was okay with the financial piece for a while because it helped me paint a more complete picture of each brand I got to work with, including everything from Jennifer Lopez to Marc Jacobs. I spent three years there because I loved parts of my job and there was plenty still to learn, but I also knew it wasn't where I was meant to end up.

I took baby steps, taking what I learned from one job and moving to the next, giving each job my all, until I eventually landed a more enjoyable and fulfilling role. At one point, I even took a senior-level job at a major record label in Los Angeles because it represented bands I loved. Working there offered me the opportunity to not only work on brands I adored, but also to perfect my sales skills.

My career has involved one pivot after another as I have

figured out how to do what I enjoy most, day in and day out.

Your professional life is just one element of leading a happy, authentic life. Personal enjoyment and discovering and acting on your passions are also key. For example, the account director at my firm loves yoga more than anyone else I know. Over time, she has learned that a daily yoga practice is essential for her to feel her best, so in addition to her career in public relations, she's become a certified yoga teacher. She loves her career, but also knows it's not enough, and that's okay. It's a great realization that ensures her days are fulfilled. This type of awareness is an important part of figuring out who you are and what matters to you.

You don't necessarily need sweeping change like a huge career revamp, a marriage or divorce, or a relocation to find happiness. Incorporating little things into your life until they eventually add up to bigger things is incredibly effective over time.

Even with these little measures, trial and error is okay—it's even to be expected. We seem to have this notion that we should *know* what will make us happy before we try it. How can we possibly know without trying? For instance, I took acting classes in Manhattan for two years. After I was done working and networking for the day, I attended night classes. I always wanted to know if acting was something that would make me happy. I enjoyed it as a kid and wanted to see if it made sense to me as an adult. Ultimately, I learned acting wasn't for me at this point in my life. I'm still glad I tried because, if I hadn't, I may have suspected that professional acting was on my roadmap, and I had missed out. And I never ever want to feel like I missed an opportunity or didn't answer a question. Again, this is trial and error—without the trial, you'll never find your way to self-actualization.

As you try out different jobs, different hobbies, and different situations, keep asking yourself questions. What allows me to feel my best *and* do my best? What brings me joy? Where do I feel the most comfortable and free to be myself? The answers to these questions will help you continue refining and taking action in your life.

MAKE A CHANGE

Some people fear asking these questions because the answers might mean that things need to change. Everyone approaches change differently. One person might wake up one day and want to change everything about their lives because they're unhappy. So, they scrap it all and start over. Another person might only be comfortable changing one small part of their daily routine to start.

However you approach it, change can be scary. It doesn't have to be, though. Change can also be gentle and gradual. In fact, often, gradual change is best.

This is particularly true when you know something has to change, but haven't yet clarified exactly what that should entail. Just because you're not happy in your job doesn't mean you should pack up your apartment and give your notice tomorrow. Often, quick reactions like this cause even more stress and don't afford you the opportunity to sit back and think about what a better scenario will look like. It certainly doesn't leave a lot of time to *find* that scenario. Also, a lot of times small changes make a big difference.

I've had a hard time fitting exercise into my life for the past three years. Between running a business, having a young family, teaching at a business school, and sitting on several boards, I literally haven't been able to find the time. So, I decided to start small by adding just five minutes of exercise to my day. At first, that meant twelve sit-ups and push-ups, followed by a quick walk with the dog. Yes, that's not what most would consider a "workout," but it was more than I was doing before, and it got me on the right track. Now, I'm able to squeeze in more and more time and prioritize exercise over other options.

Measure by measure, get yourself to an optimal situation

that slowly but surely increases your general satisfaction and well-being.

LET GO OF WHAT'S NOT WORKING

Happiness and authenticity are both contagious in a good, not flu-like kind of way. I'm sure you've seen this in your own life. People who feel free to be themselves and who have created a life they love radiate a specific brand of positive energy. They are comfortable in their own skin and at peace with life. Others want to be around them.

There are also plenty of people in life with whom we feel like we just can't be ourselves. This doesn't mean anything bad about the person; it just means they're not *your* person. Nonetheless, sometimes we keep these relationships with people who make us feel confined out of a sense of obligation, familiarity, proximity, or any other number of reasons. This can be problematic because that sense of confinement breeds bad habits. Specifically, it breeds the habit of inauthenticity.

Over the years, I've had a number of friendships and relationships that were not based on anything real. When it came time to make more time or space in my life, those relationships were always the first thing to go. There was nothing substantial holding them in place. In some cases,

I felt like I was in a constant bid to fit in or find acceptance within these relationships.

Not only is putting on a front to gain acceptance an unpleasant experience, but it also never works in the long run. There are plenty of people in the world who will not only accept but also *embrace* you for the beautiful soul you are, no matter what intricacies or quirks you bring to the table. If you aren't experiencing this sense of acceptance in your life, it just means you haven't found your people yet. Sometimes we block ourselves from this experience by packing our schedule and spending our energy on unfulfilling relationships.

Growing up as a foreigner in New York, I was always trying to change myself in order to fit in. After my stint at P.S. 81, I moved on to a private middle school, which was full of affluent Manhattan kids. Their idea of fun was shopping at Saks Fifth Avenue. Did I mention we were thirteen years old? Every once in a while, one of them would ask me to join them. I'd then fight with my mom about going out in Manhattan with these kids and dressing like them (cue $500 outfits). I exerted all of this energy when, the truth is, these shopping excursions were not necessary for me to have a full, happy life. Plus, the arguments with my mom were certainly not worth the stress they caused my entire family.

Eventually, I realized how important it is to have a genuine connection with someone before you let them into your life and allow them to impact your world. The people you surround yourself with are a direct reflection of you and the life you lead. This means there should be a selection process, as opposed to just trying to fill up time and space by collecting people.

I'm sure you've heard the saying, "It's not what you know; it's who you know." These days people talk a lot about their #squad or their #tribe. Instagram aside, the people in your life *should* function much like a squad or tribe.

Your tribe might consist of two people, or it could include twenty. What matters more than the size is the quality of your squad. You will support one another in getting where you each want to go. You will value one another's dreams and desires. You will support each other's development, both personally and professionally. You will be free to be open, honest, and direct, even during the more difficult moments. Communication will be authentic and transparent. Yes, this might sometimes involve tough and uncomfortable conversations. Those are not only welcomed, but they help you and others around you grow.

There are also some telltale signs that you *haven't* yet found your tribe. If you feel physically or mentally exhausted after being around your "friends," chances are they're not for you. Hanging on to relationships like this is counterproductive in the long run. Most of us come to realize this naturally as we get older, perhaps for no other reason than the simple fact that, as the years pass, we have less expendable time. The people and things that aren't truly important to us naturally fade away.

However, it's not *always* this easy or natural. Sometimes you have to make a concerted effort to sever ties, which can be difficult. This is particularly true in scenarios where more people than just you and the other individual are impacted by the split. For example, if you have a group of friends, but realize one of those individuals isn't healthy for you, all of your other friends are impacted as well. In cases like this, it might seem easier to allow the relationship to continue limping along.

If you find yourself in this sort of situation, think long and hard about your own well-being, and then act from there. Ask yourself if this relationship brings out the best in you. Does it contribute to an evolving, happier you? If not, it's probably time to make some tough decisions with your greater good and continued quest for happiness in mind.

YOUR PERSONAL BRAND

Your personal brand encapsulates how you present yourself, those things that matter to you most, the actions you take, the people you surround yourself with, and how you spend your time.

An important aspect of your personal brand is that it doesn't only cover the *good* parts of you. It includes *all* parts—the good, the bad, and the ugly. And we *all* have good, bad, and ugly elements of our personal brand because, again, we're all human.

Maybe you're a social butterfly who is happiest around others. Or perhaps you're more of an introvert, and social settings make your skin crawl. While it is sometimes good to push yourself to stretch outside of your comfort zone, it's also important to know who you are and what makes you happiest. If you're a jerk, embrace your inner jerk. If you're kind and compassionate, embrace those qualities. Own who you are. When you do, you'll be consistent, and people will know where they stand with you and won't be confused about your behavior.

Also understand that only *you* know who you really are. No one else can or should tell you who that is. Sure, a trusted network of people can help guide you when you need some assistance or insight, but even they can't hear what your mind and heart are telling you. Sometimes, it can be hard to listen to yourself (especially if you're not crazy about some of your qualities), but if you can just get quiet and tune out the external noise, your heart and mind will always tell you who you are and what you need to do. People can't fight authenticity—you can always defend what's real.

We've all fallen into the trap of doing what others want to do, rather than doing what *we* want to do. The problem here is twofold. First, you will never be satisfied if you're making decisions to make other people happy. Second, people have an innate sense about whether or not what you're showing them is authentic.

Being who you are will earn the trust of others. If you do something for the sake of pleasing other people, it likely won't even be effective. Sure, you've made the motions, but it won't resonate with those around you as authentic. It won't build trust. It's impossible not to respect someone who's confident in who they are, weird traits and all. You can't cover up who you are forever, so have the courage to be that person. And on a practical note, it's a lot easier to remember what you told someone when it's the truth, versus remembering the story or personality you concocted to win them over.

WHY YOUR BRAND IS IMPORTANT

Of course, you're not a brand—you're a person. I use this term because there are some important parallels between brands and how you present your authentic self to the world.

In the world of marketing, we talk about being clear, consistent, and compelling. No one is compelling all of the time, but everyone should strive for clarity and consistency. You want to clearly communicate who you are, and the thoughts, feelings, and emotions that are most important to you. When things change, be transparent and own the changes. Vagueness and obscurity are not sustainable. Authentic personal branding *is* sustainable because you have something to back it up: you. When your branding is true, you won't have to carry the stress of trying to recall what you said or what image you portrayed. There is great freedom in that.

Compelling marketing results when a brand's value proposition is different from that of their competitors. They have something interesting to offer. No one is interesting all of the time, but no matter what, you have a unique point of view, and *that* is compelling. Your value proposition, in a sense, is that you're uniquely you.

THE EVOLUTION OF YOUR BRAND

Most people want to be better, and they want to showcase themselves in the best possible light. There's nothing wrong with that, as long as your efforts are genuine and you acknowledge that vulnerability can also be a strength.

It's okay to be human, because, after all, you *are* human. The more you connect with others on that level, the easier it will become to improve, and for you to lift one another up toward more happiness and success.

Another important element of personal branding is that, just like any other brand, your brand will change and evolve over time. Who you are today may not necessarily be the person you are a year from now. Situations change, goals come and go, and the experiences you have along the way mature you.

Knowing who you are is an ongoing journey, filled with continual self-discovery. You may love something today that you disliked ten years ago. That doesn't mean you're inauthentic; preferences change. It is, however, critical to be consistent in one thing over time—always be you, whoever that is at any given moment in time.

You don't necessarily need a process for this. You don't need to be constantly monitoring yourself, running down your checklist of likes and dislikes, preferences and goals, to make sure they are still a reflection of you. The only thing you need to be is self-aware. As things change, recognize that they have changed, and remain transparent.

TRANSPARENCY IN THE DIGITAL AGE

As recently as a decade ago, your personal brand was conveyed solely through real life. Today, your personal brand and reputation extends to the life you display online. Authenticity guru, social entrepreneur, and writer Michael Simmons discusses how others often base their first impression of us on what they see on the internet. Before they've even met us in person, they've already made their decisions about whether or not to connect and how to interact with us.

In many ways, the virtual world may not seem "real." Whether that's true or not, it still has a significant impact on the real world and on our real lives. Many relationships are built online, and much of our communication happens there. When you assume an online persona, it's almost impossible to maintain that image in real life. You are not an avatar. You are a walking, talking, breathing human being.

If you've tried dating online, you know how off-putting an avatar can be when it doesn't match up with the person behind it. The relationship is doomed before it even begins. When the time comes to meet, expectations and reality don't align. There's a cognitive dissonance between perception and presence. How can trust possibly be built from this point?

What you post online is no small matter—in fact, it can

be a huge deal. You have to be able to back up what you put out there, and to verify that your online image is substantiated by your real-life experiences, thoughts, and feelings. A gap between your internet and real-life presence is one of the fastest and most common ways to lose credibility and trust in this day and age.

There are some caveats to this. Let's say you're a twenty-year-old college kid applying for a job. Your Instagram and Snapchat posts are all focused on your last fraternity rush. This is totally authentic—you love your frat, and it's important to you at this point in life. However, this image also won't do you any favors in the working world.

When it comes to your internet presence, it's important to find the balance between being genuine and remaining mindful about the impact your online image can have. Let's go back to the example of the college kid. You are authentically invested in your fraternity. However, you are also enthusiastic about starting a career, and you are particularly excited about the job you've just applied for. Which takes precedence?

Step back and think about how people are going to perceive you with no other information available besides what's available on the internet. Are you portraying a holistic version of yourself? Does your social media reflect the image and reputation you want out there in the greater world?

In the professional world, social media doesn't stop impacting your IRL reputation once you've got the job. I would guess that most of us are connected to at least some of our coworkers on social media. This is a part of life these days, but it can still get precarious.

If you wear a suit to the office and your Facebook profile picture is of you wearing shorts on the beach, of course that makes sense. No harm done. This is a natural divide between your professional and personal life. But let's say you call out of work "sick" on Friday; however, the Instagram pictures of you on the beach tell a different story. Okay, now we have a credibility issue.

The general blurring of boundaries between the personal and professional on social media leads to countless other problems. There is an obvious difference between your personal and professional life, but there should not be such a huge disparity that your coworkers grow confused about who you really are.

We have to find ways to deal with this because our online presence is not going away. Conversely, it's becoming more deeply entrenched in the world we live in and in our lives. A 2013 study by AVG Technologies showed that 92 percent of kids under the age of two have a digital footprint. And this was in 2013! Times have changed, and kids today are figuring out who they are online. That's a lot of pressure. It also means that, by the time they get into the working world, they will have decades of their personal history and online choices accompanying them as they step into the workforce.

Kids aren't the only ones figuring out who they are online. A lot of adults do the same. How we present ourselves online increasingly shapes how we view ourselves as a whole, as well as how others view us. How many times have you cringed at a picture or status update that pops up on your newsfeed from several years back? Since social media allows us to encapsulate moments of our life at any given point in time, it's going to include the moments when we're "figuring it out" and, perhaps, being inauthentic in the process. We've all been disingenuous at one point or another. Moments like this are part of self-actualization, and no one is genuine 100 percent of the time in this process. Just as in life, your online history doesn't have to be perfect. We're looking at the big picture.

Social media captures moments in our lives in a way that nothing else ever has before. I don't know about you, but I certainly never sent old photo albums to my coworkers or showed them pictures of what I ate for breakfast. We're still in the process of figuring out all of the ways in which social media and online channels will impact our real lives moving forward. For now, the most important part of this is ensuring that who you are online and who you are in real life match up.

THE ONGOING JOURNEY TO HAPPINESS

When it comes to happiness, there is no finish line. It is a lifelong journey. No matter how happy you are or how aligned your life is, there will still be days when you question your decisions. You might still have moments of wondering if there's something more out there. Happiness is an ongoing process, and it requires management. You want to strive for excellence, not perfection.

Some people just know at a very young age who they are and what they want out of life. Others don't. They need a lifetime of discovery to figure it out. That's okay. Even if your road to happiness and authenticity is long and winding (did I mention I love the Beatles?), each small realization and every tiny change will get you one step closer. It will make you that much happier.

It's never too late to start, either. New entrepreneurs are often advised to stop wasting time and just "start today." The same applies here: start now. You have nothing to lose, and a lifetime's worth of happiness to gain.

CHAPTER FOUR

Authentic Leadership

GROW, LEAD, AND SUCCEED

Yes, in all my research, the greatest leaders looked inward and were able to tell a good story with authenticity and passion.

—DEEPAK CHOPRA

Kristin Kahle is the founder of three successful multimillion-dollar businesses and CEO of Navigate-HCR. She's someone whom I consider a mentor. Despite all of her experience and success, Kristin admits that it's *still* difficult to embody authenticity in leadership roles. However, she'll also be the first to tell you that developing this skill is imperative—even if it is, at times, an imperfect practice.

Kristin is a great representative of the "new" management style. As recently as a decade ago, leadership philosophy often focused on being a boss above all else. It was *certainly* more important to differentiate yourself as a leader than it was to be genuine within your leadership role. Today, that's all changing as leaders like Kristin embrace the idea of being a leader rather than a boss.

She notes that there are a lot of great things about being a leader, but it's also not always easy; as with anything else, some days are better than others. It can be hard not to slip into the role of "boss" during difficult or critical moments when stress escalates and team members are challenging. It's also difficult during those moments when managing from an authentic place means you can't be everyone's friend.

CREATING A CULTURE OF TRANSPARENCY

As a leader, you are tasked with establishing working relationships in which everyone (including you) is encouraged to bring their best, most authentic self to the table. This means it's up to you to ensure that your work environment is transparent, which is accomplished through honesty and consistency. On days when this seems easier said than done, remember that your ultimate goal is always to lead, rather than manage.

BE HONEST

Honesty is inextricable from transparency. For those in leadership roles, this honesty must be projected both inward and outward. You have to be honest with yourself about who you are and what motivates you, and you have to be honest with your coworkers about, well, everything. Honesty paves the road to trust between coworkers, and it must extend in all directions.

It's not breaking news that the truth can sometimes (okay, a lot of times) be scary. Almost without exception, though, the sooner you get the truth out there, the better it is for everybody. This applies equally to every sort of deception, from small little white lies to the much bigger lie of putting on a mask. Deception is constantly waging a battle against time.

Transparency in the workplace requires that employees of all levels be forthright in their communication. One of the scenarios in which deception most frequently creeps into the workplace is through the process of feedback. Young managers, in particular, worry that feedback will be interpreted as criticism and create a negative atmosphere. And there's certainly some truth to that. Still, while holding back the truth might come from a place of compassion, it's still dishonest.

Holding back information that can serve others creates

barriers between leaders and employees. Not only are you effectively impeding the growth and progress of your team members by literally preventing them from getting better, but, particularly in the case of younger employees, you're robbing them of a resource they actually *want*. One of the hallmarks of the Millennial workforce is that they want specific feedback, good or bad, so they can make the changes necessary to grow and advance.

Despite your well-intentioned motives for holding back feedback, by doing so, you are withholding the tools for your employees' success. So often, employees don't even know when they're doing something wrong. If you don't tell them, how can they be expected to learn and improve? An integral part of your job as a leader is to help employees maximize their potential.

This is straightforward, but that doesn't mean it's easy. Trust me, I've struggled plenty with this precise issue myself. It's one that has often kept me up at night.

Good leaders want to inspire the best work from their employees by creating a positive work environment. In practice, providing feedback often feels like criticism. Criticism is generally counter to positivity. In effect, though, holding back criticism does not lead to a positive work environment—it leads to an inauthentic one. So, the trick is to deliver feedback in a clear, constructive way that is tailored specifically to the person you're speaking with and lets them know you have their growth and best interests at heart. *This* is how a positive work environment is established.

Another very human part of this conundrum is that many managers want to be liked by their coworkers just as much as the next person. It can be easy to conflate your employees' not liking something you say with not liking *you*. The truth is, your employees probably *aren't* going to like everything you say. Unfortunately, this is part of being a leader. However, once you've earned the trust and respect of your employees, they will understand that even news they don't like is being provided with their best interests in mind.

I'm sure you can see how there's a cyclical pattern here. You want to earn the trust and respect of your employees. You earn that by being honest and forthright.

It is absolutely possible to position negative news or feedback in a constructive, compassionate way (or in whatever way feels authentic to you). But this doesn't mean that you can dress this information up so much that it's no longer clear. Without clarity, honesty can become shrouded in such a veil that your coworkers can no longer interpret the seed of truth in what you're saying. To build transparency and trust, you have to be vulnerable with your coworkers sometimes. You display great vulnerability when you are clear and honest, which, as we've discussed, others will appreciate and connect with.

BE CONSISTENT

It is up to you to cultivate a consistent environment. Your team doesn't want to be surprised by the actions or behavior of their boss any more than you want to be surprised by your boss. (Although, if you want to surprise them with a happy hour, go for it!) People want to understand what to expect and be able to project how various situations will be handled.

This need for consistency applies to all levels of employees. However, it's especially important for managers and anyone in a leadership position. Years ago, I had a coworker who was very open about her personal life. On the weekends, she enrolled in various self-development courses, which she shared with our entire team. Our boss was also in the loop and appeared supportive. Seeing this support was a big deal for everyone. It demonstrated that not only was the focus on coursework outside of work okay, but it was also okay for us to share personal information about ourselves with one another.

Unfortunately, the minute my coworker produced work that did not meet exceptional standards, our boss blamed her extracurricular activities. He suggested that my coworker stop attending these classes so that her work was not impacted. Implicit in this was the fact that our boss was using the personal information my coworker had shared against her.

I'm sure you can imagine how drastically this changed the workplace culture. Now, instead of feeling like we worked in a safe, consistent environment where we could share personal information, we had no idea what to expect from one day to the next. My coworker particularly felt like she could never divulge personal details at work, even if it was relevant to her professional success. After all, it could be used against her. It was up to our boss to decide whether or not to embrace personal information within the workplace environment. However, once she made that decision, she should have remained consistent.

Inconsistency in the workplace erodes transparency because it robs employees of their sense of security. While your expectations may evolve over time, they should not change on a daily basis. When they do change, employees should be in the loop. As we discussed in the previous section, this information should be presented in clear, straightforward language.

Another part of consistency is making sure your team knows that the guidelines and expectations you set for them apply equally to you. In other words, if you expect employees to be honest with you, the same is required in reverse.

LIGHT THE FIRE

The topic of respect has already come up a couple of times in this chapter. That's because, as a leader, one of the most important jobs you have is to earn the respect of your team. What this means in the workplace is changing.

Just as so many of the other elements of working life have evolved over the past couple of decades, so has the idea of what it takes to be a good leader. The old approach to management was that it didn't matter if you were liked within the workplace. It really doesn't have to be lonely at the top anymore. In fact, it probably shouldn't be.

Once upon a time, common sentiment held that there should be a huge divide between bosses and employees. There was almost a sense that employees should fear their managers and leaders. Take a look at established companies, and you can usually see at least some degree of the remnants of this hierarchal philosophy.

Today, this sort of structure is viewed as increasingly ineffective. It's certainly true that separation and fear don't exactly breed a collaborative environment. With traditional hierarchies within business, the leaders are alienated from the rest of the pack. Really, leaders and their packs should be engaging with one another.

This doesn't mean that all employees will look at their mangers and leaders as peers, necessarily. While a paycheck is important, what many young employees crave just as much is experience, collaboration, motivation, and inspiration. As a leader, you have the incredible opportunity to provide this inspiration. Strive to be the leader who lights the fire within, rather than the one who cracks the whip.

You want your employees to *want* to do better for you. While fear might provide results, it's not the best motivator. With fear, there can be no team spirit. There can be no investment. You will likely not see employees advance from good to excellent to great. Instilling respect and inspiration, on the other hand, will generate all of these things.

THE HUMBLE LEADER

You will be the best leader when you bring your authentic self to work, and lead from that unique place. However, it's also worth mentioning that humility is a quality that many great leaders possess. When you are humble, you also have the opportunity to put some of the vulnerability we've talked about into practice.

It can be easy to stagnate once you reach a certain level. This is a disservice to yourself because there's always more to learn. It's just as important that leaders ask for help when they need it as it is for anyone else in the company. In doing this, you also establish a culture in which others are not afraid to do the same. Everyone has the opportunity to keep on growing and learning from others. Not only this, but those who do have the knowledge someone else needs have the opportunity to step up to the plate, which is a great confidence builder.

Today, when I need help, I ask for it. I wish I'd learned how to do this earlier in my career. As a young manager, I never wanted to show my cards. I certainly didn't want to ask for help, because I thought that made me seem weak or unintelligent. I thought that if I couldn't solve every problem by myself, my team would lose faith in me. It took me years to realize that one person can't move a mountain. There was no way I—or anyone else, for that matter—was going to have all the answers.

This is precisely why teams are so important. Everyone has their strengths, and not all of our strengths are the same. Teams rise higher together when everyone is transparent about needing help.

When I was in my midtwenties, I secured a job at a record label as the director of sales. Despite the fact that I had little sales experience and had never worked in the music industry before, I was thrown into a situation where I was in charge of a team of national sales representatives. I knew I could do the job, but the first three months were some of the toughest I ever faced in my career. Not only did I have to figure out a new job, but I also had to lead a team of people who had a lot more industry experience than I did.

My team members were in their thirties and forties, and most of them had grown up in the music industry. I was leading people who knew a lot more than I did, and it was a humbling experience. I was in LA, and my team was spread throughout the country, so most of their questions came over the phone. It seemed that the majority of the time, my answers were of little help to them. I spoke off the cuff, and I told them whatever I thought they wanted to hear. I realized this strategy was not going to work in the long run, and I took a very necessary step back.

I thought about my worst-case scenario. What would *really* happen if I admitted I didn't have all of the answers to my team's questions? Would they think I was incompetent if I didn't know everything? Or was it actually an opportunity for us to solve problems together? I figured the answer was probably the latter.

From that point forward, I changed both my mindset and

my actions. When I didn't have answers, I acknowledged that. It was scary, but I also knew that it was a better option than the stress I'd been living under.

Once I acknowledged to my team members that I may not have the same vantage point as them—or the same experience—everything seemed to move in the right direction. I explained that I would do whatever it took to get them what they needed, and we worked on solving issues together. My mindset shift improved the work environment for everyone involved. It also taught me a good lesson in the importance and power of humility as a leader.

ASSERTING AUTHENTIC AUTHORITY

Anyone can be given a management title. However, you cannot force your employees to *view* you as a leader. The right to lead can only be earned. This right is earned by creating trusting, healthy relationships with your employees. As you know by now, healthy relationships are created through genuine actions and authentic behavior.

If you've ever had an inauthentic or inconsistent leader, you probably know how difficult it is to respect or want to do a great job for them. Not only that, but it's extremely difficult to run a successful company with leaders at the helm who say one thing and do another.

One of my mentors, Tammi Terrell, a former vice president at AT&T whom I worked with, taught me the importance (and power) of creating an open, welcoming environment, free of fear and dictatorship. Through her example, I learned how critical it is to be accessible to your team. Of course, this doesn't mean that you have to be available all of the time, since you will never get any work done. It *does* mean that you ensure you are approachable for employees of all levels, and that you provide those you manage with what they need to be successful.

As a leader, it's also very powerful to gain an understanding of both your team members' professional *and* their personal goals. This will help you understand each one as a whole person. When employees understand that you view them as people, not just staff, they will respect and trust you all the more. Also important in understanding your team members as unique individuals is recognizing that everyone shouldn't be managed in a one-size-fits-all mold. This requires some genuine conversations and the ability to truly listen. You don't have to be friends with everyone who works for you, but you should find a way to connect with each and every one of them and know what drives them.

You also have to let your employees see and get to know *you*. You have to let them know how you work best and what you expect from them. It's also okay to let them know that you, too, are human, and you're not perfect.

No one is 100 percent authentic all of the time, and that includes even the best leaders among us. The goal here is to have fewer of these inauthentic moments. Recognize when you're being inauthentic, and ask yourself why. Hold yourself accountable. Demonstrate for your team what it means to be authentic, even if that's as simple as not telling a white lie to a solicitor on the phone just to get out of it the easy way.

Some days this is easier than others. I strive to connect with my team in an authentic, human-to-human level every day, but I'm not always successful. However, on the really good days when I feel like I understand my team and they understand me, we move mountains. We work smarter and faster. We make big strides together as a united front.

THE FOUR PRINCIPLES OF AUTHENTIC LEADERSHIP

Andreas Jones, CEO of Battle Tested Leadership, got it right when he wrote that authentic leadership finds its roots in ancient Greek philosophy. At the heart of each of the four principles of authentic leadership that follow below are the qualities Greek philosophers held so dear— fortitude, temperance, justice, and prudence.

PRINCIPLE 1: BE FLEXIBLE

Authentic leaders don't get locked into a single way of doing or thinking about anything. They have the ability to understand each unique person and situation, and to adjust accordingly. For an authentic leader, genuine communication comes before all else.

PRINCIPLE 2: COMMUNICATE DIRECTLY

Authentic leaders understand how to cut directly to the core of an issue. They don't dance around it or dress it up as something it's not. They get straight to the point so that everyone can get on the same page and know where they stand.

PRINCIPLE 3: EMBODY YOUR VALUES

A leader must embody their values both inside and outside of work. As we've discussed, the lines between our personal and professional lives have never been more blurred than they are today. You get to choose what your values are, but once you own those values, you must also embody them for your team. Words mean nothing without action to back them up. And nothing destroys authenticity more than saying things you don't really believe or live up to.

According a 2016 *Forbes* article entitled "12 Habits of

Genuine People," sincere leaders are far more effective at motivating people because they inspire trust and admiration through their actions, not just their words. As the article puts it, "Many leaders say that authenticity is important to them, but genuine leaders walk their talk every day."

PRINCIPLE 4: LEAD WITH YOUR HEART

Leading with your heart doesn't make you weak. It makes you strong. It also requires vulnerability, which allows your team to connect with you, and to understand that you're a person, too. That's a *good* thing.

These four principles are at the core of every single leadership quality we have discussed throughout the course of this chapter.

DEVELOPING GREAT LEADERS

Most promotions are triggered by milestones. That milestone might be mastering a skill, achieving a specific goal, or obtaining a certain number of years under your belt. Or a promotion might come because you've proved yourself on the job or gone above and beyond to demonstrate your mettle.

One thing people are generally *not* promoted for is their ability to be genuine or to personally connect with others.

It's unfortunate because these are the skills of great managers. The fact that someone has demonstrated they're ready for "the next step" doesn't necessarily speak to their capacity to be a good leader.

Often, people are thrown into leadership roles with little to no management experience. In this scenario, it makes sense that they figure out how to lead by looking at their own managers and emulating how they handle relationships. The problem here is that their managers may very well have been promoted for similar reasons, rather than for an innate ability to lead well.

This is how we end up with leaders working under the assumption that they must create distance between themselves and their subordinates in order to command respect. Leading from this place makes it quite difficult— if not impossible—to rally your people behind you. It creates distance rather than solidarity.

Big companies often use online learning tools for management training. This generally consists of lots of modules to be completed and boxes to be marked. There are sexual harassment modules, office design modules, and sales modules. These days, there's an online learning module for pretty much every aspect of the working environment. I'm sure you can guess what's *not* a common module (yet): authentic leadership.

According to a *Harvard Business Review* article entitled "The Truth about Authentic Leaders," this is a critical oversight. Here is how they see it:

> "Research and leadership development programs should focus on how leaders develop their authenticity. Being authentic as a leader is hard work and takes years of experience in leadership roles. No one can be authentic without fail; everyone behaves inauthentically at times, saying and doing things they will come to regret. The key is to have the self-awareness to recognize these times and listen to close colleagues who point them out."

Younger companies are adopting a different, nonmodule approach to management training and leadership development. Of course, a significant part of this involves focusing on their products and services. However, many startups are also highlighting their corporate culture as a key to success. They strive to create an atmosphere where people want to work, where they want to do their best and exceed expectations. A key component to this is leadership and transparent culture.

This approach is informal, yet it's proving to be a serious advantage for startups. Larger, established companies haven't caught on to this idea yet. Companies who figure out how to incorporate authentic leadership into their training, whether through modules or another form of education, have a huge leg up in the market.

Ask any sales rep what makes them successful, and they'll say it's their relationships. They probably have every CRM program in the world reminding them of clients' birthdays and pinging them to follow up on a lead, but the relationships they've cultivated over the years are what closes the sale at the end of the day. The only way to cultivate these genuine relationships is by *being* genuine.

With so many organizations lacking specific programs that train employees in authentic leadership, we need to get creative and figure out our own ways to incorporate authenticity into the workplace. Right now, one of the best ways is to learn by example. There are plenty of leaders out there who are committed to a transparent culture, where people are encouraged to be vulnerable and to express who they are. We can learn from these leaders.

Some people are not interested in showing their cards at work. They show up, do the work, keep to themselves, and go home. Maybe these people are successful in certain environments, but most businesses today require that their employees give a little. You have to let your guard down. If we expect employees to do this, we, as leaders, must be willing to do the same.

If you know you can be more transparent with your employees, but can't figure out exactly where to start or what that looks like, begin by looking at your environment. If you're fortunate enough to work in a business that supports transparency, you have the opportunity to learn from others. Ask them to coffee, take them to lunch, get to know them, and ask questions about how they do their job the way they do it. Transparent people are open to this sort of initiative, because they want to bring out the best in everyone.

If you find that you're having many inauthentic moments, ask yourself why. Are you in an environment that doesn't support transparency? If so, you can be the change-maker. Cultivate authenticity one person at a time, beginning with your direct reports. All it takes is one person to begin an entire movement; that means you have the power to shift behavior in measurable ways.

Of course, huge transformation doesn't happen overnight, and that's okay. Start with yourself, and lead by example. You'll notice that your employees become more engaged and get more out of their workday because they're more connected to one another. They will begin to stand out from other teams in the company. That, in and of itself, will speak volumes.

Part of your professional development is refining your

understanding of what you want out of your career. It's about being vocal about your goals, and managing up. So many people fail to adopt new approaches and new ways of being because they simply assume that their boss will never support them. Don't assume this. Your boss is human, too. Your boss may very well want to see the same changes and advancements you do, but may not know how to go about achieving them.

Often, people who get stuck in "the same old way as always" haven't even asked for support to enact change or growth. You have no idea what others are willing to do unless you ask. Know what you want out of your career, and use authenticity as a key differentiator.

HOW INAUTHENTIC LEADERSHIP BACKFIRES

It's impossible to feel secure at work when you're afraid of your managers. It's also very difficult to feel engaged and to see the big picture of why you're doing what you're doing. You might stick around for the paycheck, but chances are you won't actually enjoy your work experience.

This is a bad situation for you, but what many managers fail to see is that it's bad for them, too. People who are less engaged are also less productive. They are afraid to voice their opinion because they fear being shut down, think they won't be heard, or are concerned that something they say will be used against them. In this type of environment, creativity suffers. When employees are afraid of leadership, they're more willing to leave the company. They face uncertainty on a daily basis because they don't know what to expect when they go to work. Sure, they can sustain this environment for a while, but it always catches up to them. With high turnover comes increased pressure on the remaining employees, which makes them less likely to stay, too, and negatively impacts products and services. It's a bad whirlpool of a cycle.

Employees in a transparent environment are free to let their creativity fly. Even if their ideas are not used, they know that their contributions are valued. This makes them think about what else they can add to the conversation. They're excited about work. They're excited about being part of a collaborative team. They're motivated, they perform better, and they keep contributing ideas. *This* is a positive cycle. *This* is the cycle you want to promote as a leader.

AUTHENTIC LEADERSHIP IN PRACTICE

Tammi Terrell was one of the first female leaders in the telecom industry. When she started, she was the only woman at the board table. Now she's one of hundreds.

Much like the rest of the country, Tammi's staff was

greatly impacted by 9/11. Fear, lack of trust, and chaos were pervasive as the company prepared emergency communications. In the midst of this difficult time, having a culture of trust was essential. Tammi encouraged her team to be honest about why they couldn't come to work, and she respected their personal requests. Establishing this sort of environment in the wake of disaster, when people needed it most, enabled Tammi to build even stronger connections with her more than one hundred employees. Her approach resonated with them, it made her human, and they wanted to work harder and do better for her.

When you work in an environment where people cannot be straightforward about their wants and needs, and they don't feel heard or recognized as individuals, honesty suffers. We see this when people call in sick because their vacation request is not granted, or because they were out late the night before. We've all done this at some point, especially in our younger career days. However, when it's a chronic scenario, it's a red flag that points to a lack of connection and respect within an organization.

Regardless of what sort of environment a leader facilitates, an employee might not always be granted the time off they request. However, when authentic leadership is in place, both parties will be able to communicate more openly and easily, and employees are less likely to lie.

Even if an employee doesn't get what they want, they know that calling in sick would be a violation of your trust, which they value. They will understand that even if they didn't get what they wanted in this particular scenario, it was for a valid reason. This is why authentic dialogue between managers and their employees is so important—everyone is impacted by the relationships you build with your team members.

I once managed a junior employee who was new to the organization. Our policy was that on Fridays we worked from home. I was clear with everyone that my expectation was they would actually *work* from home and it was not a travel day. We also asked that they remain within twenty miles of the office in case a client or manager unexpectedly needed them onsite.

The idea behind this was to reward employees on a weekly basis by sparing them the time and energy of commuting. We wanted them to save time on their commute and also feel like they could start their weekends early by having a less stressful Friday.

This junior employee decided to bend the work-from-home rules; she didn't see the harm in working from a different remote location. Rather than asking her manager if she could use the day for travel or telling her manager she would be on an airplane, this employee assumed no one would notice and went about her plan. After all, she could get a Wi-Fi connection on the plane. Unfortunately for her—and everyone she worked with—the connection was down. We tried in vain to get in touch with her for four and a half hours. No response. Meanwhile, this woman was panicked for the entire flight because she realized her plan had backfired and, in the process, she had broken a core company value—transparency.

If she had told the leadership team she needed to travel that day, they would have figured it out together. Someone would have perhaps delegated her a task that didn't require an internet connection, or given her half of the day off so she could travel in peace. Because she was new and didn't understand the environment (which the company also has to take some accountability for), she failed to realize that open communication is more important than anything else. She thought keeping her plans under wraps was worth the risk, because what if her manager didn't understand her side and give her the travel time? It was a hard lesson for her to learn, but it reinforced why honesty, open communication, and respect is so important in the workplace.

Sometimes even a solid relationship built on trust doesn't always compensate for a lack of quality communication. Here's a common scenario: a perfectly responsible employee goes out of town without thinking through or planning for all of the potential fallout. As a result, the rest of the team picks up the slack. Of course, you could resolve this by issuing a warning when they return or putting a performance plan in place. These measures are generally overly extreme, though, because most employees don't have negative intentions in this sort of situation.

A better resolution would be to have an open conversation. (Of course, if this situation happens many times, it's a different story.) From this, employees can learn how to do better in the future. Leaders can also continue to grow by honing their constructive dialogue. Through collaborative effort and healthy communication, relationships can improve, your work environment can became stronger, and you can grow as a leader.

YOU ARE TEACHING OTHERS HOW TO LEAD

Being a leader isn't always easy. But being a *good*, authentic leader is always worth it. In doing so, not only do you grow as a person, but you help others grow, too. You teach them how to lead through example.

As a leader, you set the tone for the team. You become a role model for the type of leader your team members will become. This is both a big responsibility and a huge opportunity. I encourage you to seize it—even in the more difficult moments.

CHAPTER FIVE

An Authentic Culture

A WORKPLACE WHERE
EVERYONE THRIVES

Authentic brands don't emerge from marketing cubicles or advertising agencies. They emanate from everything the company does.

—HOWARD SCHULTZ, CEO AND EXECUTIVE
CHAIRMAN OF STARBUCKS

It wasn't long ago that I started hearing new titles in the workplace—director of creativity, vice president of culture, and so on. These are markers of a noticeable shift in the corporate environment, a deviation from the old-school way of business.

One of the reasons these types of titles began to pop up

was because companies started searching for ways to engage their employees. This new focus made it clear to culture-focused companies that employee engagement was a specific, full-time job. Someone needed to own the work of organizing teams as a united culture. This can't fall under the umbrella of a human resources director, who is bogged down with the daily tasks of hiring, training, dealing with benefits, and handling any day-to-day issues that arise. You can think of a vice president of culture as someone who represents the company's *esprit de corp*.

I'm sure it's not totally unrelated that, in 2018, Kimpton Hotel & Restaurant Group, LLC was ranked the sixth of 100 Best Companies to Work For by *Fortune* magazine. Kimpton employees cited a culture of inclusion and acceptance as one of the things that made Kimpton stand out from other employers. (Personalized welcome packages for new hires and the allowance of pets in the workplace also topped their list of favorite things about Kimpton.) With this, 95 percent of Kimpton team members said that management trusts them to do a good job without watching over their shoulder. Ninety-four percent feel that coworkers care about one another. And from my perspective, the most impressive stat of all is that 96 percent of Kimpton employees feel that they can be themselves at work.

CULTURE TRICKLES DOWN FROM THE TOP

Kimpton couldn't be as beloved by employees as it is today if leadership wasn't truly invested in their employees as individuals. This trickles down from leadership, specifically from the company's founder, Bill Kimpton, and CEO, Mike DeFrino, who are both known for being genuine and engaged. For better or worse, leadership lays the groundwork for corporate culture. Team members shape and mold it.

By now, it won't come as a surprise that there are two common denominators in great corporate cultures. These two qualities are consistent across the board, regardless of the sector or size of the business: authenticity and transparency. As we discussed at length in the previous chapter, leadership is responsible for allowing these two qualities to thrive in the workplace.

When we're thinking about culture, it's important to distinguish between a good culture and good perks. Just because a company has good benefits doesn't mean they have a good culture. Cayan CEO and cofounder, Henry Helgeson, did a great job of clarifying the difference between these two things in a *Mashable* article titled "7 Steps to a Happy, Authentic Corporate Culture." Hegelson talks about how leaders have to genuinely embrace the culture they want to create, and then take ownership of the creation process. This is accomplished, he says, by encouraging employees to be themselves, and to voice their opinions without fear of being reprimanded.

Healthy corporate cultures are born when people can be themselves, are encouraged to voice their opinions without hesitation, and are inspired with a clear sense of the company vision.

Perks and benefits are great. But without the elements Hegelson mentions in place, no amount of perks will make employees feel truly satisfied.

CHARACTERISTICS OF AN AUTHENTIC CORPORATE CULTURE

Three elements are inextricable from a good corporate culture. With the skills you've honed in the previous chapters in mind, establishing or contributing these to your company will be a much easier process.

TRUST

Trust is one of the main ingredients of an authentic corporate culture. When you trust your coworkers at every level, you have the freedom to be who you are, and to ask for help when you need it.

A UNITED FRONT

With the ability to be yourself at work, it should feel safe and natural to lean on your coworkers. This will take different shapes from one company to the next. In some companies, teams will lean on one another solely for professional reasons. In others, coworkers will turn to each other for both professional and personal purposes. The specifics of what this united front entails are not as important as the feeling of being supported by one another and knowing that you're in it together.

A POSITIVE ENVIRONMENT

It's easy to assume that a positive work environment follows when trust and support are in place. This is often—but not always—true. It might feel authentic to some companies to run on a high level of stress. For other companies, what is authentic to the majority of employees is a terse demeanor that still manages to include trust and support.

Among the three characteristics of a good corporate culture, a positive work environment is the most intangible. However, I'm sure we can all agree that we know it when we see it.

THE AWKWARDNESS OF AUTHENTICITY

Leading business software and project management company Asana is doing something right. Valued at $900 million as of 2018, the company puts values first and product second. It employs more than three hundred very happy people and has one of the best workplaces around if Glassdoor (a website on which employees rate their employers) is any indication. One of Asana's leading taglines is, "We're empowering teams to do great things together." While that certainly speaks to their product that helps streamline and organize businesses, it's also how they find success internally.

Just a few years ago, Asana was a small startup. But they were a startup with a clear plan. People started noticing Asana very quickly based on their high ratings in a variety of metrics. They achieved a 4.9 out of 5 rating on Glassdoor. *Fast Company* cited Asana as having the best company culture in technology. Both of these accolades are likely based on the fact that Asana encourages its employees to bring their whole selves to work. However, this is only the beginning of why employees love Asana. The main draw seems to be that team members are encouraged to take responsibility in a way that is unparalleled, and self-awareness and curiosity are deemed essential.

Asana's cofounder, Justin Rosenstein, has helped build awareness about authenticity as a critical element of corporate culture. Rosenstein talks about the importance of authenticity this way:

"I consider tolerance for awkwardness one of my competitive advantages. A lot of both personal and professional relationships are impeded by people being scared of being truthful...But if you can just stay present with the awkwardness and see it through to the other side, and remember that everyone's on the same team, you can get to the truth. And the truth can let you go faster in whatever you're trying to do."

Rosenstein makes an important point. Authenticity doesn't come easily; it can be tough to achieve. It creates awkward conversations that aren't comfortable. However, it also creates genuine, trusting relationships. With that, you can work through anything—including awkwardness.

MUST-DOS FOR AN AUTHENTIC CULTURE

A transparent culture doesn't just make for a better work experience. It's also considered a best practice in the most successful businesses.

So what are the best practices, the "must-dos," for an authentic workplace culture?

ATTRACT AND RETAIN THE BEST EMPLOYEES

There are countless benefits to an authentic workplace culture. At the top of the list is the fact that this type of environment attracts and retains the best people. Companies with an authentic culture have happier, more engaged employees. The more engaged employees are, the less likely they are to leave.

In her article "The Negative Impacts of a High Turnover Rate," published in the *Houston Chronicle*, Miki Markovich writes about how an organization's mission is lost when it is constantly hiring and training new employees. She suggests that businesses can lower their turnover rates by providing adequate training, rewarding employees, and creating a company culture of trust. At the end of the day, people want good benefits and compensation, but they also want to feel secure and comfortable at work every day. Trust goes a long way.

To establish trust and work to their maximum potential, shared core values have to exist among employees. When others can understand and relate to your core values, collaboration naturally follows. We do our best to only hire and recruit employees who have the same core values as my company. I have found this sort of united vision results in the most inspired work and atmosphere.

HIRE FOR CULTURE

Building a successful team requires finding those people who are a good representation of your company and what it stands for. There are few things I love more in my professional life than hearing someone tell me how much they love one of our employees. Regardless of their position, every single team member represents the overall culture of a company. They *are* the company.

When you're building anything—whether it's a department, a division, or an entire company—it's important to remember that every single person involved plays a critical role. If core values are not aligned, situations have the potential to turn ugly quickly. Just one person is capable of making or breaking an organization. That person probably won't be there long, but a lot of havoc can be wreaked in a short amount of time.

Since I run a boutique-sized firm, it's important to me that every team member interacts with job candidates. In the course of these meetings, we've developed a set of questions designed to get to the heart of a candidate's core values. Over the years, we have refined these questions.

In our first year of business, our interview questions were pretty basic. We asked candidates about their background, characteristics, and experience. As time went on, we realized that what we were looking for had less to do with a candidate's answers, and more to do with how they approached their response. For example, when someone shows vulnerability in their answers, I immediately bump them to the top of my list. And the more specific we can get about how they handle difficult situations, the better.

In the course of interviewing, we try to bring out as much of the candidate's personal interests as possible. Sometimes, we take the interviews out of the office to see how the person interacts with others. Are they kind or rude to their waiter? Are they patient? This gives us a glimpse into how they will be at the office. Since one of our core values is positivity, if a candidate can't handle a situation in a positive manner, they are probably not a fit for us. The most important things any employee brings to the table are their values and authentic self. Personal interests reflect both of these things.

I recently asked a candidate to identify three things she

would do with her life if money wasn't an issue. This is a tough question in the context of an interview because candidates are trying to demonstrate they want to work. Through this question, I was trying to identify those things that are most important to her in life. Her first response was she would spend time with those who mattered most to her. That showed me that she values relationships, which is a crucial part of our internal and external work. In fact, that's another one of our core values. She also discussed her passion for learning and helping others grow, which let me know she's invested in others and not just herself, which is a great leadership trait. I see these sorts of values overlap with candidates, and I'm more open to their past experience.

It's important not only for you to get to know candidates throughout the interview process, but also for them to get to know *you*. Be transparent about what the culture and job are like so that candidates can make an honest assessment of whether or not it is a good fit for them. For example, some people thrive in a nimble, fast-paced culture; others prefer more order and predictability. One isn't better than the other, but it's important that employees have a realistic understanding of what daily life will look like. Frank conversations will allow candidates to determine if this job is likely to be satisfying for them.

While a candidate's skillset is obviously also important,

there have been times when we hired people who did not have the exact skillset for a position because they were a perfect cultural match—specifically, their focus on results and sense of urgency. My philosophy is that we can always change a title for the right person and find a more fitting role that still aligns with our business goals. I believe that if someone has those qualities, they'll be successful if we find the right position for them.

Last year, for instance, our team was looking for an account supervisor to manage certain accounts and lead media outreach. It took a little under two months for us to narrow the pool of candidates down to our perfect match. And yes, that's faster than normal, but that goes back to our sense of urgency. The woman we hired was a great fit for our culture.

Once on board, our new account supervisor's first couple of months were challenging. She lacked the media relationships necessary for the position. Nonetheless, I saw so many awesome qualities in her and was determined to figure out a way that would work for all of us.

The account supervisor and I sat down and devised a plan. We engaged in an honest conversation about what she wanted to do, and what the company needed. Then we put our heads together to figure out how to bridge that gap.

Within six months, we changed her role. She joined the operations team as a managing director. This was a completely different job than what she'd been hired for, and a much better fit. She blossomed in her new role and has become an integral part of our company, helping create processes that enable us to scale faster and be more efficient.

REMEDY HIRING MISFIRES

No matter how refined your hiring process is, it's impossible to make the correct decision 100 percent of the time. Things move quickly, and work needs to get done. However, when a hiring choice backfires, it's important to fix it right away. When you're dealing with someone who has the potential to be a culture killer, you must be direct and transparent in your approach.

If you have come to realize that the employee isn't coming from a place of authenticity and isn't in line with the core values, it may be time to part ways. You can teach someone a job, but you can't teach transparency or change someone's attitude. If they're unwilling to be authentic or take accountability, you can't force it.

One of the main core values of a team I worked on many years ago was going the extra mile. "Good enough" didn't cut it at this company. A fellow team member wasn't a good fit with this culture. She was better suited for a job that allowed her to clock in and out. This was a difficult match with the other six team members who had a shared desire to keep on working until a job was done right. We relied on each other to excel as a team. Unfortunately, we quickly learned that we couldn't rely on our coworker. Communication broke down as a result, and our work atmosphere shifted from positive to negative. It created distance between us and her, which I'm sure was an unpleasant experience for our coworker as well.

Our manager at the time was forced to have a direct conversation with this woman about the company's expectations, and the fact that she wasn't meeting them. When approaching conversations like this, it's important to remember that you don't know what else might be going on in a person's life. I believe in giving employees the chance to turn a situation around.

As second-in-command, I connected with the employee and asked her to have an honest conversation with herself and figure out if she even wanted to step up her game. If the answer was yes, we would be thrilled to continue moving forward with her. If not, it was time to part ways. In this case, after taking some time to consider her ideal work situation, this woman decided she was not capable of what we needed, so she found a new opportunity.

Once she left, the work environment returned to its previous positive state. Corporate teams are a lot like sports teams—everyone has to show up ready to play with all they've got to win the game. If one person isn't willing to do what's necessary to win, the team will flounder. All it takes is one weak link.

MANAGE, AND SET GOALS

A culture runs smoothest when the individuals within it feel like they're seen for who they authentically are. Acknowledging individuality lies at the heart of managing and goal-setting in a way that promotes a great culture.

I make a habit of asking people how they like to be managed when they join our team. Some people prefer a lot of attention, including daily check-ins and a task-oriented approach. For others, it is important to have the freedom to find their own way to accomplish goals. Friction results when you manage people in a way that doesn't resonate with their personal style. Having an open conversation about preferences keeps team members happy and the culture much more positive.

I like to set annual goals that encompass both the company as a whole and each team member's personal and professional goals. We do this by beginning with business goals and then establishing a business plan that incorporates employees' goals. Including personal goals within this framework allows me to understand my team members even better and to gain insight into what's important to them.

For instance, we have a junior staff member who has never been to Europe. One of her personal goals for the year is to travel abroad. Knowing this allows the team to support and root her on, as well as to plan around her probable two-week absence.

Another employee included her desire to work on new business sales as part of her annual goals, despite the fact that sales is not part of her position. We have supported her decision in doing this, as well as coaching her through the process. Once a month, we check in to see how she's doing, and have discussions about who she should reach out to, the type of presentations she should put together, and the events she should attend.

Understanding your employees' goals offers yet another inroad for connecting and demonstrating your investment in their success, both personal and professional. Bringing the whole team on board fosters a supportive environment, which allows everyone to win.

EFFECTIVELY DEAL WITH WORKPLACE ISSUES

Even in the best workplace cultures, issues are going to arise every now and then. The best way to deal with issues of any variety is with genuine, direct conversation. I think these conversations should occur as quickly as possible once an issue presents itself.

Problems have a way of escalating when they are not handled efficiently and directly. Team members begin to chatter, and opinions—not to mention imaginations— can run wild. Almost before you realize it, a molehill becomes a mountain. This works in much the same way a grudge does. It doesn't just go away over time. Instead, it continues to grow until it either explodes or is resolved.

Jumping on coachable moments offers another advantage, too. Even if you think you can fix a problem as time goes on, people forget how they felt or precisely what they were thinking in a particular moment. If you don't jump on the matter immediately, often an opportunity is lost.

MAINTAIN ONGOING DISCUSSION

No matter how busy you are or what's waiting in the pipeline, one of the most important tasks on your list should always be clarifying changes and expectations to keep team members on the same page. This ensures the ongoing health of your corporate culture. It eliminates confusion.

As time goes on, project directions will change. The company will grow and evolve. Expectations will shift. All of this is to be expected. However, when you fail to maintain an open dialogue about expectations in the midst of change, it leaves room for team members to start reading between the lines.

Continue discussing the vision of the company. It helps everyone keep the bigger picture and purpose in mind. This creates a united goal and, with that, a united front. It also allows team members to share any thoughts or ideas they might have about how best to achieve those goals and visions.

To maintain your transparent culture, you have to share not only the good news, but also the bad. When the news is bad, it's all about framing. And remember to always frame discussions of any variety as "we." Together, we win and we lose. Together, we have one vision.

COACH AND MENTOR EMPLOYEES

My good friend Kristin Kahle is masterful at investing in her employees in powerful ways that improve both their professional and their personal lives. She puts a lot of effort into understanding their challenges and struggles and addresses them in thoughtful and powerful ways. Recently, Kristin explained to me why this is so important to her:

> As CEO, I get to impact employees' lives every day. I am able to see my impact on so many of my employees, since I give them the freedom to thrive. If I was not open and honest and authentic, my employees would not be able to grow, not only personally, but also professionally.

It's important for Kristin to create a culture where people are comfortable being vulnerable. Since she has established this sort of open culture, no one fears being reprimanded for sharing their challenges. As a result, everyone has the opportunity to grow and learn together.

At Crowe PR, we frame this philosophy as the core value "do better, be better." This means we always strive to do something better than the way we did it last time. This includes always being a better person than we were before. Every day should be about some form of improvement, no matter how small.

One of the best ways to keep improving on a consistent basis is to have a trusted guide, coach, or mentor. A great leader will build this into their role, or they will identify someone who fits the bill. It's so difficult to look at things objectively when you're in the thick of it. A coach can help with challenges, identify solutions, and create a plan to get you headed in the right direction.

I meet with Kristin every month. In our monthly meetings, we discuss the current challenges I'm facing personally and professionally. She then breaks these challenges down and rearranges them in a way that offers me a new vantage point I was unable to see before. This relationship and these conversations alone have helped my business grow.

As an experienced leader, Kristin also meets with my employees. She takes the time to establish a trusting relationship with them, and then works with all of us to close any gaps she notices that will stand in the way of our success. She takes the time out of her insanely busy schedule to help us be the best we can be.

ATTRACT AND RETAIN THE BEST CLIENTS

Similar to our focus on hiring the best people, we view clients as an extension of our internal team, and they see us as an extension of theirs. To do our best work, it's important that we resonate with our clients and strategic partners, and that our worldview aligns with theirs. Thanks to our transparent culture, it's easy to screen out organizations who aren't a good match for us, which is in everyone's best interests.

This approach is helpful not only in a service industry like ours, but also in *any* company-client relationships. At the heart of every transaction is a relationship, so the two parties need to trust one another, or their business involvement either won't go smoothly or won't stand the test of time.

Shared values break down barriers. In practice, they ensure that no matter what, the partnering companies will figure out how to have a great working relationship. After all, you already know you're on the same page about the most important issues.

AN AUTHENTIC CULTURE IN PRACTICE

As many companies do, our team has a standing meeting every Monday. We begin with everyone sharing one thing that they're particularly grateful for that week. Most of the time, it has nothing to do with their professional life. When it does, they often talk about being grateful for a big win, a great opportunity, or perhaps a team-bonding event.

It's great to hear when a team member's professional life makes them happy, but there's no expectation that the discussion centers around work. The meeting is designed to provide an opportunity for everyone to open up and engage in genuine conversation. It allows us to understand where our coworkers are coming from as we head into the week. It's so helpful to start Monday with a positive framework, and to gauge everyone's mindset before the work begins. It's also a great tool for remaining mindful about maintaining our corporate culture on a regular basis.

Our Monday meetings include our core values in the agenda, as a way of reminding everyone who we are, as a team. It's also a forum for open discussions about what's working and what's not. We've put a lot of work into ensuring that people feel it's a safe space to share their thoughts.

If you cultivate trust, an open environment, and a safe space at work, everything can be communicated. Everyone can feel that they have a place at the table, and your culture will thrive.

CHAPTER SIX

Brand Authenticity

KEEPING IT REAL

The keys to brand success are self-definition, transparency, authenticity, and accountability.

—SIMON MAINWARING, AUTHOR OF *WE FIRST*

Branding creates the public perception of your company. A great brand will feel familiar and be consistent, even as time passes and products evolve.

As most people know, Steve Jobs was a marketing and PR genius. He was also one of the greatest innovators of our time. Steve Jobs's identity is so entwined with Apple that when people think about Apple, they think about Steve Jobs. It follows, then, that when people think of Apple, they think of innovation. This is their brand. Brands include products, but they also include the talent, mindset, and culture of a company. Everything we've talked about in this book so far plays an integral role in a company's brand.

Branding serves both an internal and external purpose. For employees, a company's brand serves as their rallying cry; it is the promise that everyone is achieving as a unified front. Your company's brand is also part of how you represent yourself to the world as an individual. For example, if people know you work for Google, they will assume that you are intelligent, forward thinking, and dedicated to innovation. Those are the qualities that Google stands for. If you say you work for Facebook, people will have a different perception of you than if you work for General Motors.

From an external perspective, brands are the image of a company that the public sees. It's how the public connects and builds a relationship with a company. The public includes customers, of course, but it also includes potential employees and partners.

About 30 percent of the cover letters I receive from potential job candidates begin with something along the lines of, "I've been following your company on Instagram for quite some time, and I love what you guys do." It still surprises me because we're far from the biggest players out there. But we're transparent, we're genuine, and we like to work hard, have fun, and celebrate one another and our clients, which is obvious from our accounts.

When you decide where you want to work, you have to ask yourself if you believe in the company's brand value and promise. It's more than just buying into the company's culture—it's also about believing its brand. After all, the result of your work is what you're putting out into the world. If you're environmentally conscious, you may feel a lot better about working for Tesla than a gas-guzzling SUV plant. You have to be able to connect to the company's brand, and to believe in it.

WHY BRANDS MATTER

Brands are how businesses communicate with people. They are how a company differentiates their products and services from everyone else's. There might be twenty-four different types of water on the shelf at the grocery store, but there is only one Evian.

Marketers spend millions of dollars on branding, perfecting every detail from the brand's colors to its font to its message. Essentially, they are creating an identity. Part of that brand identity is a personality. Just like people, some brands are mysterious or sexy. Others are clever or whimsical. Some are friendly, while others are elitist.

While a lot of thought, strategy, and money go into building a brand, it's also not something you can create without substance. Brands have to be an authentic reflection of the company and the people that create the product. Consumers have an innate sense of what is and isn't real when it comes to branding. They won't trust a brand if they don't believe it. It's difficult to run a successful business when customers don't trust you. Today's consumers have plenty of other options to choose from, and they will generally select the brands that feel most trustworthy.

Right now, companies have so many more touch points with consumers than they did ten years ago. It used to be that big companies created relationships through one primary mode: advertising. A company would spend a million dollars to create and produce a beautiful ad that was sent out to the masses through television, print publications, and packaging. Since the process was finite, it was much simpler to keep brand messaging consistent.

There are more opportunities than ever before for people to get to know a brand, but there's also much more pressure on companies. A consistent message is key, and that message must maintain its consistency across many different and varied platforms. Brands today must meet the challenge of being compelling, clear, and consistent over the long term, on a lot more customer-facing platforms than ever before.

GUARDING YOUR BRAND'S AUTHENTICITY

You may have heard the saying that it takes thirty years to build a reputation, and thirty seconds to destroy it. Success, reputation, and trust are not built overnight. And while ecommerce and social media are enabling more and more businesses to get in front of customers directly, the road to brand loyalty is still long and winding.

Fads and overnight sensations don't stand the test of time. Fads can create a nice spike in revenue, but they don't build a sustainable business. For businesses, sustainability trumps a moment of glory every time. Not only do you have to work to build trust, but you also have to make an ongoing effort to keep that trust. A random error in judgment, or what seems to be a harmless mistake in branding, can eradicate trust and destroy a business's reputation.

I think that, at some point, most business are tempted to move away from a strategy that's worked for years. This impulse is often triggered by a competitor's sales spike. Before making any knee-jerk reactions, consider what this change might do to your reputation. Think about your loyal customer base. They've been with you so far for a reason. They've already bought into your company and what it stands for. Messing with that sustainability for results you cannot predict and that are not guaranteed is a risky move.

Outside of crisis-type moves, there's no quicker way to

destroy your brand's authenticity than by being wishy-washy and inconsistent. If you want to jump on the green-washing movement and promote sustainability, yet you have not actually supported this initiative in the past, you can't claim it without creating a credibility issue. As a general rule of thumb, if you're not doing something, you shouldn't be talking about it.

It's okay to make some shifts over the long haul, as long as they are authentic to your brand. However, constantly changing things up only serves to confuse the marketplace. Who *are* you, anyway? And how can all of these different versions of you be authentic at the same time?

There are so many ways to identify a brand—think of all the brand logos, trademarks, and mascots that have stuck in your mind over the years. When you see a gecko on a banner at the airport, you automatically know you're looking at a Geico advertisement. Geico has been very clever with this strategy because they know it works and makes their brand identifiable. They're not trying to add a duck in the mix just because AFLAC has one. That would just be confusing.

YOUR BRAND CONVEYS YOUR MISSION

Brands that hop around from one end of the spectrum to the other are generally not focusing on conveying information about their mission to consumers. A big part of brand authenticity is the inclusion of your company's mission and core values. For a brand to be authentic, it must represent your company's mission. Clever advertising and marketing are great, but it's your company's mission that will make your brand unique from competitors.

A couple of years ago, Southwest Airlines launched an entire campaign that revolved around the idea of transparency. (Or, as they cleverly put it, "transfarency.") I, obviously, love this! The premise of the campaign is that Southwest considers transparency about their fee structures to be of the utmost importance. Their tagline is, "Low fares. Nothing to hide." At transfarency.com, where the campaign is housed, Southwest compares their prices to those of their biggest competitor, Spirit Airlines, on a line-by-line basis. This campaign very effectively reinforces the idea that transparency builds consumer trust.

Your company's internal vision, mission, and goals should be aligned with your brand's external message. To do this, your vision and mission have to be substantiated by action. If you say you're one of the best places to work, where's your evidence? Your claims have to be based on something.

SHARE YOUR STORY

Public relations gets a bad rep sometimes. Many associate it with the entertainment industry and "spinning" everything. While people and companies absolutely do pull stunts to bring attention to themselves, I would argue that PR can be incredibly authentic when tackled from a storytelling perspective. Storytelling provides an effective inroad for letting an audience know and trust a company or brand, no gimmicks necessary.

Brands are often built around a story that grows from the seed of the company's mission or core values. It is through these stories that companies convey the things that matter the most to them, and that set their brand apart from the rest.

A solid brand can make an ad feel like a story. This is important, since your customers will have a much more emotional and human connection with a story than a blatant brand message. Of course, all kids love stories. But even as adults, we tend to respond better to anecdotes than lists and details. Stories stick in our brains and are easier to recall. Facts are generally in one ear and out the other, along with all of the other information we ingest on an hourly basis.

Conveying the essence of your brand through storytelling allows you to tap into a consumer's range of emotions.

It allows you to—here's that word again—*connect* with customers. Your story can be conveyed as a narrative, yes. However, your story can also be told or used as a through line in everything from your business cards to your packaging.

This is how brands become beloved. There are only a handful of those truly beloved brands in the world today. You know who they are—companies like Google, Disney, and Amazon. This love is a powerful resource to have because, with it, it becomes almost impossible to bring down that brand. To become beloved is a lofty goal, but it should be the ultimate goal for any company or marketing team.

While stories are a great inroad to make a memorable connection, they have to be *good* stories that are told well. Virgin Group's chief marketing officer, Ian Rowden, once said, "The best brands are built on great stories." I wholeheartedly agree.

Sometimes, people get overwhelmed by the idea of coming up with a story for their brand. It seems like there isn't one. I'm here to tell you, there's *always* a story. The biggest trick is positioning your story in such a way that it will resonate with your specific audience.

Maybe you have a highly technical product that you're

selling directly to consumers, or in the B2B space. At first glance, it might seem like a story isn't appropriate—or even feasible—in this situation. In truth, a story can actually be quite helpful in scenarios such as this because it's likely that your competitors won't use this strategy. A story becomes a way of setting you apart even more than stories normally do.

Perhaps your story explains how your company came to be, or how the technology was developed. How did you come up with the idea in the first place? How have you seen this product improve results or otherwise change the game for people in your audience's field? With this tactic, you are ensuring that people will remember *your* brand, as opposed to simply reading—and quickly forgetting—yet another product description.

All of this isn't just supposition. It's science. According to One Spot research referenced in a *Fast Company* article entitled "Why Our Brains Crave Storytelling in Marketing," 92 percent of consumers want ads to feel like a story. It's our job, as company leaders and PR firms, to deliver that content in a clear narrative, in whichever form is most effective. That might mean a video, article, advertisement, or some combination of these mediums and more.

There's a lot of noise out there, and consumers have a

ton of options. You have to differentiate yourself not just through your attributes, but also through your ability to emotionally connect in the process of conveying pertinent information.

OWN YOUR BRAND'S UNIQUE ATTRIBUTES

Marketing 101 tells us that companies have to create value for customers in order to get value back. One way to create this value is to offer a product or service that is better or different from that of your competitors. Maybe you have a safer car or a faster computer; or perhaps your price is lower and you offer more options. Your company creates value, and your brand captures that value for consumers so your company makes money.

There's something unique about every company, even if plenty of other businesses offer similar products or services. Where is your value? What is different or unique about you or your product? What makes you better? What's your competitive advantage? You have to clearly communicate these answers to your customers.

This goes back to the idea of presenting a clear, compelling, and consistent message. Clarity is achieved when your message isn't diluted, and the customer isn't confused. To be compelling, you have to be better than other brands in some specific way. Consistency recognizes that consumers' attention spans are not what they once were. There's no room for messaging that's all over the place.

Value is sometimes intangible, especially in the case of brands that have an aspirational component. A customer who purchases a Maserati, for example, derives value from the experience of actually *buying* the Maserati. It's an external symbol that indicates, "I've made it!" Even if your product isn't a Maserati, it's likely it will offer something to your customers that is more than just the function the product or service provides.

CREATING PARTNERSHIPS WITH OTHER BRANDS

In an effort to stand out, a lot of companies are creating partnerships and aligning with other like-minded brands. Cross promotion is a great way to elevate brands to the next level.

A few years ago, Red Bull and GoPro teamed up in a campaign called Red Bull Stratos. They partnered together to have high altitude skydiver, Felix Baumgarter, jump from a capsule lifted up by a high altitude balloon to a height of 120,000 feet. Felix set a world record that day. In the course of doing this, he also happened to deliver a powerful brand message for both GoPro and Red Bull. GoPro gets people out in the world (or out *of* the world, in this case) to find adventure. Red Bull gives people wings and defies them to redefine what's possible.

The right partner for your brand doesn't have to have your exact message or mission, but there does have to be some similarity. As you can see in the Stratos example, GoPro and Red Bull don't have the same message. But they *do* have complimentary messages that are aligned with one another.

When you're looking for partners to align with, you must have a clear understanding of their mission and outlook. When you put your name beside another brand, that brand's actions can have a huge influence on your reputation—for better or for worse.

The process of figuring out issues of alignment is a lot like finding the right employees for your company. You have to make sure their core values are at least similar to your own. Time and time again, we've seen big brands drop athletes and celebrities the minute their personal actions misalign with the brand.

This is very common in the world of celebrity endorsements—when brands back artists, musicians, celebrities, or athletes, they separate themselves in the midst of controversy. It's not an exaggeration to say that, in instances like this, their brand is at stake. Sometimes, the damage is already done in these situations, despite the company's best efforts to remove themselves from the scandal. When companies seem inauthentic, customers get confused. The minute you confuse your people, a door opens for competitive brands to step through.

CONNECTING YOUR BRAND WITH CUSTOMERS

Brands have many opportunities to connect with customers, and vice versa. If you have any doubt about this, think about our president. Love him or hate him, social media completely transformed our connection with the most powerful person in the country. We have more access and visibility than ever before.

At a recent digital conference, a speaker discussed the time he invested an hour on the phone with the customer service department of a major credit card company. In the course of this hour, he accomplished nothing, but wasted his valuable time, so he took to Twitter to rant about his experience. He tweeted about how he was frustrated with his credit card company, and that their customer service sucked.

Within minutes, a major competitor tweeted back at him. "We're so sorry you're having so much trouble with our competition," they wrote. "How can we help you?" They jumped on the opportunity to deliver a clear message and to create value. In doing this, they told the customer everything he needed to know about the difference between their brand and their competitor's.

People who once were unreachable are now just a post, tweet, or DM away. There are transparent battles online between the president and celebrities, and between everyday people and celebrities. We can communicate directly with almost anyone now. Moreover, they can communicate directly with us.

This type of visibility can be really helpful if you are strategic about making it work to your advantage. However, you have to be careful with this kind of visibility. What you say and when you say it matters. It's much easier than ever before to destroy your reputation in less than 140 characters. For example, in 2009, a couple of Domino's employees posted videos of themselves doing disgusting things to the food they were preparing for guests. The videos went viral, with more than one million views. This is not to mention the various mentions, repostings, and discussions they spawned on other forms of social media. The *New York Times* even picked up the story, writing, "Consumer perception of the brand had turned negative within hours, and online forums continued to discuss the videos, which were cut, re-worked, and re-posted hundreds of times, long past the apology." Every brand wants to go viral. But not like this.

Let's concentrate on the positive, though. In the marketing world, visibility is always an opportunity to deliver your message and convey your value. It's an opportunity to showcase your brand and what it stands for. Every online opportunity should be seized.

As Domino's oh-so-clearly demonstrates, it's important to think about the people who will be representing your brand on social media. If an intern posts for you, you have to make sure they are aligned with your core values and represent the company well. I had a very direct conversation with a former employee once because she made a lot of small grammatical errors in her social media posts for our company. We're in the communications profession. If our posts are grammatically incorrect, no one will hire us. If we can't make it through one post without an error, *I* wouldn't hire us.

Whenever you speak on behalf of a brand, it's important to bear in mind what the brand stands for and how best to communicate that. Every touch point at your disposal must be aligned with the brand's voice and story. Take a minute to pause before you type. Really align yourself with the brand before you communicate on its behalf. It's almost as if you were talking with a person in an attempt to catch their vibe. Remember, you *are* the voice of the brand as far as consumers are concerned. If that voice confuses consumers, they will move on to a brand that is more clear and consistent.

USING PR TO COMMUNICATE AUTHENTICALLY

At its core, the basic function of public relations is to build and maintain a brand's reputation and to create trust. If people don't trust your brand, it won't sell over the long term. You may have a quick win, but that will only take you so far.

Public relations connects companies with the media, manages their relationships with social media, and creates compelling stories that genuinely reflect who the company is. We get to the heart of the company rather than simply promoting it as you would in general advertising. Having said that, there are more and more gray areas between advertising and social media. More regulations are being put in place all the time for bloggers and influencers promoting products. These regulations are a clear reflection of the changing landscape.

Once upon a time, media outlets and interviews, announcements, press releases, and events were the primary ways for brands to paint a picture of their company for the public. Online communications add a lot of other options into the mix. You can showcase your brand in a million different ways, including social media, your own website and those of influencers, and company blogs.

When you're creating a content strategy for social media, make sure it's aligned with your company's vision. Never create a cyber alter ego for a quick win. Yes, it will take more characters to tell a genuine story. And the truth is, you could probably come up with content that is more flashy and exciting as the alter ego. However, the difference is that the alter ego's version isn't real and true. Yours is. As long as you have a good market offering and a good story, you'll be able to communicate that and earn consumer trust.

THE RISE (AND NOISE) OF SOCIAL MEDIA

According to the digital marketing agency Omnicore, as of 2018, five hundred million tweets are sent per day. That's a lot of tweets. It's also a lot of noise. No single consumer can process all of that information. And this is just one platform! As more and more social media platforms emerge, and as more and more people convert to mobile sources, it's overwhelming to even imagine the amount of information that will soon bombard us.

So how do you win this information race? To put it simply: you don't. You *can't*, barring an extremely extenuating (and likely somewhat accidental) situation. The best solution is to create more engaging posts, less frequently. Yes, you're fighting for real estate, and yes, you want to be part of the conversation to the greatest degree possible, but that doesn't mean that you have to insert yourself on every single outlet, whether it supports your brand image or not. It doesn't mean that you have to post so regularly that you're diluting your message. You need a strategy, so you don't talk just for the sake of talking. Be an active listener and base your strategy on what you're hearing.

Between Twitter, Instagram, Facebook, Snapchat, LinkedIn, YouTube, and all of the other forms of social media outlets available, there are so many options and ways to engage with consumers at your disposal.

Of all of these platforms, video tends to be the most engaging. However, this doesn't mean that video is the best way for *you* to reach *your* customers. Where are your customers engaging the most frequently? Where are they having the most meaningful conversations? LinkedIn? Twitter? Maybe it's Instagram?

After you figure this out, you need to consider the value you're bringing to the table. If a video isn't a great fit for your message, you're much better to post in another form. If you're not generating value and telling a story, people will tune you out and wait for something better to come along.

THE POWER OF ALIGNED INFLUENCERS

Before there were social media influencers, there were marketing influencers. These were the people who were able to deliver a brand's message to a target customer. By nature, influencers are respected, listened to, and admired. They could move the needle for any brand based on their reputation.

There is presently a surge of social media influencers— millions of them, potentially connecting you to millions of people. In fact, according to a study by Statisco there will be an estimated 2.77 billion social media users around the globe by 2019. This number will only continue to multiply.

Social media influencers represent an opportunity for brands to share their voice, their images, and anything else to a large audience at any time. Influencers win big, too, because they've found a way to monetize this opportunity. What started as a mom blogger movement, wherein stay-at-home moms and dads reviewed products, quickly turned into paid endorsements by product manufacturers. Suddenly, bloggers had a revenue stream from their social media activity.

As platforms like Instagram emerged, people didn't even need to write reviews anymore. All it took was a photo of a brand to get paid or receive free product. This represents an entirely new way to make a living—a way that's very appealing to some people. Some full-time influencers can charge thousands of dollars for a simple product placement. Then there are the outliers, like Kim Kardashian, who, according to Gizmodo, charges $30,000 per tweet or Instagram post. Love her or hate her, with a reach of more than 120 million followers, it makes sense that she can command this sort of price.

Influencers can work *against* a brand, too. For instance, when Kylie Jenner tweeted that she was no longer using Snapchat following a system upgrade that she didn't like, the company lost $1.3 billion in stock market value. This is the power of influencers today.

Not everyone was born to Kris Jenner, though. There are also microinfluencers who don't have a huge following, and who are not asking for millions of dollars...yet. They promote content, and they appear genuine as they incorporate the products into their lifestyle.

In return, brands are committed to sending them products. We do it, too. We have an entire marketing program that works with microinfluencers and nanoinfluecners to showcase how our clients' products can be incorporated into people's lives. Our team has to make sure our clients stay on brand with their updates and upgrades, and that they don't alienate key influencers. Every action still has to be genuine, and in line with the brand. There are a lot of elements to consider to pull all of this off in a way that works.

BRAND AUTHENTICITY IN PRACTICE

Now that we've looked at the scope of brand authenticity, let's see how it works in practice.

One of our clients, the leading barefoot shoe company, VIVOBAREFOOT, does a great job of getting their message out. The company's founder, Galahad Clark, is a seventh-generation shoemaker from the multibillion-dollar Clarks's footwear dynasty. He based VIVOBAREFOOT—which literally translates into "live barefoot"—on the premise that shoes have been made with the wrong approach for the last several hundred years.

Galahad's ideas were formed based on some of the very first people who inhabited the world, the San Bushmen of Africa. Their thin, flat sandals served the singular purpose of protecting their feet from the elements, such as hot sand and thorns. Galahad believes that shoes should be foot-shaped and wide, thin, and flexible. They should allow you to be grounded, move better, and have healthier feet. In addition, he is passionate about sustainability. He incorporates this ethos into everything from the materials used to create his products to a design that better connects you to nature and the environment.

Having grown up in an industry that holds views very different from his own, Galahad decided to form his own company. He initially established Terra Plana, which eventually evolved into the VIVOBAREFOOT of today. The founding belief of this company is that everyone is placing their feet in, as Galahad calls them, "foot coffins."

I've sat through countless interviews with Galahad during which journalists ask him about his brand. Every time, Galahad brings up this idea of foot coffins at some point. Here he was challenging an entire established industry in the course of his response. From a PR standpoint, this can be tricky.

Nonetheless, Galahad is so genuine in his passion that it's easy to see why people have embraced the brand. The company walks the talk, making dozens of different shoes for men, women, and kids, all designed around healthier movement and using better materials, including algae, corn, recycled plastic—you name it. Thanks to Galahad and the team he's built around him, VIVOBAREFOOT is making a big impact on its industry and society not only by educating other footwear companies on how to make more sustainable products, but also by giving their customers and brand ambassadors something to rally around. His brand could not be more authentic.

Galahad has a deep understanding that authenticity is

something that is earned over time, but that can be lost very quickly. His story demonstrates that when you're authentic, you remain true to the standards you've set for yourself, and success will always find you, no matter what obstacles you encounter along the way.

Conclusion

Be who you are and say what you feel because those who mind
don't matter and those who matter don't mind.

—DR. SEUSS

When I was much younger, I didn't understand why
people would put on an act instead of just being themselves. Over time, I've come to realize that sometimes
people have a hard time being who they are for fear of
judgment, or because of their own uncertainty or inse-
curity. It can be hard to understand that you can't go
wrong by being genuine in *every* scenario. But once you
begin to truly grasp this concept, everything changes. You
get better, you lead better, your working environment
improves, and even your business does better.

Trusting your gut and staying true to the ideals that are

important to you will always lead you in the right direction—even if it doesn't seem that way at first. Sure, you might encounter some difficulty along the way. That's life. Still, staying on the path that feels most genuine to you and having real conversations is always paramount. Doing this will arm you with the tools you need to connect with other people in such a way that you can understand what matters to them, and they can understand what matters to you. There's no difficulty that can't be overcome when we are authentic.

Inauthentic behavior might make you feel "safer" in the moment. What it really does, however, is prevent success and decrease your ability to operate to your full potential.

People cannot fault you for saying how you feel. Communicating what you want and who you are and providing honest feedback is the best way to engage people in your company. It all starts by being transparent. Everyone won't always be happy with what you have to say, but you'll build their trust and respect in the long run. It's the long run that matters.

BE GENUINE AND CONSISTENT

To engage employees and pique the interest of customers, you have to be genuine and consistent—do what you say and say what you do. You don't—and shouldn't!—have the answers for everything. View those moments when you don't know as an opportunity to ask for help, and to strengthen your connection with your team.

I'm sure it's not surprising to you that authenticity is one of my company's most important core values. Another big one is continuous improvement. It's important to all of us that we always strive to be better and do better. In our profession, we're often asked how we can guarantee results. We can't guarantee an article will be printed or the amount of media coverage a client will receive in a year; there are just too many factors outside our control. What we *can* guarantee is that we will plan to win, use all of our experience, continuously innovate, and work as hard as anyone possibly can to get our client the results they need and that we'll be a trusted partner they can continue to grow with.

I'm grateful for all the great things our clients say about us—but it's not just because of the results we bring. It's because of the trust and confidence we build. We become partners, and we're aligned with our client's goals. It's important that everyone succeeds in the relationship.

A WORKPLACE IS FAMILY

This is how we work as a team, too. We're a work family. Every Monday morning when I hear someone say they're grateful for an opportunity their job presented them with or for their team, I'm proud that we've been able to create an environment people love to work in. Naturally, each day presents new challenges and opportunities. But knowing that team members have a sense of purpose, understand our shared vision, and want everyone to succeed shows what's possible with trust and transparency.

Every company is different. Only you and the members of your leadership team can determine the type of corporate culture that best suits your company. What works for us is setting people up for success.

Transparent corporate cultures create environments where people are unafraid to voice their ideas, opinions, challenges, and opportunities. "Managing up" is a phrase you'll often hear within our walls because we want people to share their thoughts. Managers then know what their team is trying to accomplish, and no one becomes frustrated and leaves the company.

People need a safe environment that allows them to buy into their company's vision. Everyone, including the company as an entity, operates most efficiently when everyone is aligned, engaged, and feels they can voice their opinion freely.

COMMUNICATION IS KEY

Communication breakdown is the cause of pretty much every major problem, whether it's in a personal relationship, politics, or a corporate environment. Without good communication, gray areas and confusion result, leading to bigger problems down the road.

Fostering an environment of two-way communication is essential. You can always get a pulse on how you're doing by asking your team open-ended questions. This doesn't mean that your door is always open for anyone at any time. Set your boundaries and be clear about what works for you. If you set the precedent that it's okay to have hard conversations, people will work more comfortably—and better—because they won't be afraid that speaking up will cost them their job.

ALIGN FOR CHANGE

No matter the present state of your job, your work environment, or your brand, there's always room to be positive about how it can change and evolve. I believe positivity is contagious. Life is better when we're doing something we love with an optimistic mindset. I've found that I'm significantly more fulfilled when I'm aligned with who I am and what I want to be doing. Align yourself, and I'm willing to bet you can make changes far greater and more extensive than you might presently imagine.

It takes practice to be aligned, just like it takes practice to be optimistic day in and day out. Some days are easier than others. Some days are downright difficult. If you know in your heart that you are unhappy with your current situation or aren't where you want to be, the changes you take to get to a better place don't have to be drastic. I can't make drastic changes in my life. I have financial, social, and family responsibilities that prevent me from doing so. However, I know that every day I can take steps toward becoming more aligned with who I really am and what I truly want to be doing. This gives me the power to accomplish anything I set my mind to.

THE AUTHENTIC WAY

I'm the first to admit that it's hard to be authentic in every single situation. There is a good reason why white lies exist—in the moment, they make life easier and less awkward. Sometimes we tell ourselves a "little bit" of inauthenticity is necessary to spare someone's feelings or to keep moving forward.

Every day I come across situations where I think it would be a lot easier to take the inauthentic route. If I make that choice, though, at the end of the day, I'll be bothered by the fact that I wasn't true to me and to who I know I am.

Not too long ago, I was grocery shopping at Trader Joe's

with my sons. As I was loading the groceries into the car, I noticed a bag of celery that I forgot to pay for. Now, if you have two small kids, I'm sure you can imagine how annoying it is to spend an hour in the grocery store, walk back to the car, buckle everyone in, and then realize you have one package of unpaid-for celery staring you in the face. The easiest thing would have been to keep moving and chalk it up to a lost dollar for the grocery store—a dollar that the store would never even miss.

I considered my options for a minute. Finally, instead of getting in the driver's seat, I said, "Oh no! We didn't pay for the celery." My boys asked what we were going to do next. I really wanted to tell them that it was just a dollar, and I would settle our account by paying an extra dollar the next time we came in to Trader Joe's. But I knew that saying that wasn't *really* the easy way out. I would continue to be bothered by the fact that I was acting against what I felt we needed to do.

"All right, everybody, out of the car!" I said. "We're going back in." We spent another fifteen minutes waiting in line, and we paid the ninety-nine cents for our celery. I got my penny, returned to the car, and the situation was over and done with. I wouldn't have to think about it anymore. I did what felt right and genuine to me. It was just a bag of celery, but I knew the message I wanted to send to my sons, and it wasn't about taking the easy road. Anything less than that would have been inauthentic.

The same principle applies when I'm on a call and my team can hear me—if I were to say something untrue, I'd be setting an example that little white lies are okay. Everyone has a different definition of what constitutes a little white lie, and what's okay and what's not, but I'd rather remove all ambiguity and be as authentic as possible.

It's important to remember that all of this is a process. You can't just turn authenticity on and off. Like most important things in life, authenticity is something you have to continuously work on. While authenticity seems like the simplest thing to achieve because you're basically listening to yourself and your needs, the reality is that it takes time and dedication. As you learn how to be your genuine, natural self, you'll instill this ability in others around you as well. That's a pretty big payoff.

Working on your personal authenticity means surrounding yourself with people who make you better and who lift you up. From a professional standpoint, authenticity is about working in an environment that suits you best and that is aligned with your core values. In leadership roles, it's about understanding that genuine communication is integral to developing trust among the team.

Take steps to catch yourself when you're being inauthentic and become more aware of the situations in which you find yourself acting in a way that's not really you. Ask yourself why this happens, and figure out how to shift your behavior and outlook. Isolate the problem, and take the necessary steps to do the right thing and to be genuine the next time you find yourself in a similar situation.

It's about continuous improvement and knowing that you have the power to do anything. If you're part of a culture that's inauthentic, change it. If that doesn't work, you also have the power to change your situation. There's no reason to be stuck in a position that doesn't feel right to you. Take small steps and find the place—literally and figuratively—where you can thrive in every way.

As a leader, it's important to understand that every person is different. You should treat everyone uniquely and communicate with each person in a way that fits their style and approach. No matter what, if you're genuine, honest, and transparent, you'll form the best connections possible, and you'll build trust in every aspect of your life.

For as scary as all of this might seem, remember that at the end of the day, authenticity is your biggest asset in every realm of life. Being authentic sets you apart from everyone else. It allows you to bring something different and unique to the table. It allows you to bring *you* to the table. You're the only person who can do that.

About the Author

ANNA CROWE is founder and CEO of Crowe PR, a bicoastal public relations and influencer marketing agency. She has spent nearly twenty years working for iconic brands in New York City, Los Angeles, and San Diego, pivoting from an auditor position at a Big 4 accounting firm to leading and scaling her own business. Anna teaches marketing classes at the University of San Diego's School of Business; serves as comanager for Changemaker Chats; and sits on the board of the San Diego chapter of the Entrepreneurs' Organization. A former Moscovite and longtime New Yorker, Anna lives in San Diego with her husband and two children.

Made in the USA
San Bernardino, CA
02 January 2020

62590771R00105